Creating CityCenter

WORLD-CLASS ARCHITECTURE
AND THE NEW LAS VEGAS

Creating CityCenter

WORLD-CLASS ARCHITECTURE
AND THE NEW LAS VEGAS

WILLIAM R. SMITH | SCOTT J. TILDEN

with LYNNE LAVELLE

W. W. NORTON & COMPANY
NEW YORK · LONDON

For information about permission to reproduce
selections from this book, write to
Permissions, W. W. Norton & Company, Inc.,
500 Fifth Avenue, New York, NY 10110

For information about special discounts for bulk purchases,
please contact W. W. Norton Special Sales at
specialsales@wwnorton.com or 800-233-4830

Manufacturing by KHL Printing Co. Pte Ltd
Book design by Chin-Yee Lai
Production manager: Leeann Graham

Library of Congress Cataloging-in-Publication Data

Smith, William R., 1952–
Creating CityCenter : World-Class Architecture and the New
Las Vegas / William R. Smith, Scott J. Tilden ;
with Lynne Lavelle. — First edition.
pages cm
Includes bibliographical references and index.
ISBN 978-0-393-73366-2 (hardcover)
1. CityCenter (Las Vegas, Nev.)
2. Architecture—Nevada—Las Vegas—History—21st century.
3. Las Vegas (Nev.)—Buildings, structures, etc.
I. Tilden, Scott J. II. Title.
NA6216.L37C587 2013
720.9793'135—dc23

2013015111

ISBN: 978-0-393-73366-2

W. W. NORTON & COMPANY, INC.,
500 FIFTH AVENUE, NEW YORK, N.Y. 10110
www.wwnorton.com
W. W. Norton & Company Ltd., Castle House,
75/76 Wells Street, London W1T 3QT

2 4 6 8 0 9 7 5 3 1

CONTENTS

INTRODUCTION

The initial vision for CityCenter grew out of a small meeting in February 2004. MGM Resorts International President, Chief Financial Officer, and Treasurer Jim Murren called me into his office to discuss his ideas for creating a world-class resort on a parcel of company land between Monte Carlo and Bellagio on the Las Vegas Strip. He envisioned a mixed-use project encompassing urban streets and parks, multiple hotels, convention centers, luxury retail stores, condominiums, office buildings, and an extensive art program. He thought that the Strip needed a "center," a place for people to visit and experience a modern city's excitement. Jim directed us to be forward looking in the creation of a twenty-first-century city with environmental sustainability at its core.

Over the next seven months we hired a team of urban planners and created a master plan along with preliminary budgets and a timeline. As the master plan took shape, we realized that we were about to embark on the creation of the single largest world-class destination resort—with an area of 18 million square feet—in only sixty months. We subsequently received approval from the MGM Board of Directors to begin the selection process of its architects and designers.

To fully grasp the magnitude of creating CityCenter, you must imagine the necessary coordination of the countless activities that accompany concurrent design and construction of separate buildings, along with that of complex road, bridge, and utility infrastructure and a highly efficient central plant. Our master plan called for the separate engagement for each structure of a world-class architect, consultants, contractors, subcontractors, vendors, suppliers, and property managers. Project-wide communication would be key, requiring monthly executive meetings, often with over a hundred people in attendance, and countless more informal coordination meetings each day. The cash flow needs and the construction accounting requirements for CityCenter were equally daunting, with hundreds of millions of dollars to be accounted for, and paid out, nearly every month. Finally, we knew that from the venture's outset the daily movement of materials and of nearly 12,000 construction workers to and from a limited site would present unprecedented logistical challenges 7 days a week, 24 hours a day. CityCenter would test everyone!

Creating CityCenter provides an illustrated journey through the genesis and execution of the largest privately financed building project in U.S. history. The book's photographs capture each development phase, from study models and concept renderings to construction and openings.

This book also features profiles of key individuals who participated in City-Center's formation. Their stories convey the excitement and major challenges involved in its construction. In most cases, CityCenter was the largest undertaking in their professional careers.

We wrote *Creating CityCenter* to provide you with an insider's view of the conception, construction, and operation of this mega-project. It includes spectacular photographs taken during the course of the project, as well as keen, firsthand insights recounted directly by those who participated in the daily management process. This book is a tribute to the thousands of individuals who made CityCenter possible. Without their commitment and dedication, CityCenter would not be open and thriving today.

We organized the book's chapters chronologically, starting with the history and early development of Las Vegas. In the second chapter, we discuss MGM's evolution. The three following chapters cover CityCenter's master planning, construction, and architecture and interior design. The last two chapters focus on landscape architecture and CityCenter's opening activities with the operations team.

We invite you to read on and explore the exciting and intriguing story of *Creating CityCenter*. It is a tale filled with commitment, challenges, and plenty of high risk, as well as a tale of how MGM's daring vision and a team of professionals and workers created one of the most remarkable and stunning resorts in the world in only 1,825 days.

Welcome to CityCenter, but be sure to wear your hard hat—it is a busy job site!

BILL SMITH

Chapter 1

EARLY HISTORY OF LAS VEGAS

From the first settlers to brave its inhospitable climate in the early 1900s to the millions who visit its casinos each year, Las Vegas has always attracted and rewarded those who take a risk. Its history is a great American story, filled with luck and happenstance, and formed by pioneers of industry, engineering, and business. The city owes its transformation from desert oasis to gaming capital of the world to early federal projects such as the railroad, nearby Hoover Dam, and improved water sourcing, as well as to the persistence of its population growth, which closed the twentieth century as the largest in an American city founded in that century. Today, the 4.2-mile stretch of Las Vegas Boulevard known as "the Strip" is home to the largest hotel and casino resorts in the world, and a prime tourist destination. Winners and losers, innovation and failure, shaped a pattern of creative destruction that redraws the map of the Strip year after year.

There was a time when it was illegal to flip a coin in Nevada. On March 19, 1931, however, the state voted to legalize gambling and overturn a 1910 state law that had driven the industry underground. The country was in the grip of the Great Depression, which had led to population flight from this relatively young state and a tax deficit for its much-needed public schools. As the first state

Las Vegas' first housing was 64 bungalow-style cottages, which were built in 1910 to house railroad workers. Though some of the cottages still stand, their original occupants were laid off en masse in the mid-1920s, when operations moved to Caliente, Nevada.

in the union to allow casino-style gambling, and with large-scale construction projects under way nearby, Nevada spent the remainder of the decade largely insulated from the effects of the crumbling national economy. Las Vegas was now—officially—in business.

The first seeds of the Strip were sown on April 3, 1941, when California hotelier Thomas Everett Hull opened the El Rancho Vegas Hotel on Highway 91. An instant success, the low-rise California Mission–style complex spanned 63 acres and featured 63 guest bedrooms, an outdoor swimming pool, a cocktail lounge, stores, a 250-seat dining room, and not least, a 300-seat casino. Its striking tower sign, topped by a neon-lit windmill, drew weary motorists and Hollywood stars alike, and its amenities were a mix of glitz and kitsch, with horse riding, a no-jacket-required evening dinner, and a featured live show by the "El Rancho Starlets" dance troupe, accompanied by a live orchestra.

The El Rancho was preceded by the club Pair-O-Dice (1930) and the roadhouse Red Rooster (1931) on the highway, but was the first facility to be built within the parameters of the Strip. It began a building boom that saw the Last Frontier, Flamingo, Club Bingo, and Thunderbird casino-hotels open by the decade's end, each more ambitious than the one before.

El Rancho's desert location inspired Texan resort and movie theater–chain owner R. E. Griffith and his nephew William J. Moore to open the Last Frontier Hotel one mile to the south on October 30, 1942. Griffith and Moore purchased the 35-acre 91 Club site (once the Pair-O-Dice), in an attempt to attract northbound motorists before they reached the El Rancho. Designed by Rissman & Rissman Architects, the Last Frontier tempted travelers with a roadside pool and front casino, and took El Rancho's Old West theme even further with Pioneer-style furniture and memorabilia in its courtyards and rooms, costumed staff, and rodeo riding. It later added an adjacent reproduction town named the Last Frontier Village, and the hotel became the site of Las Vegas' first wedding chapel, the Little Church of the West.

By the mid-1940s, Las Vegas' burgeoning resort industry had begun to attract the attention of organized-crime figures, among them New York's Benjamin "Bugsy" Siegel. A lieutenant for crime boss Meyer Lansky and his associate Charles "Lucky" Luciano, Siegel had been charged with overseeing the outfit's national horseracing wire service in California before being redeployed

The famed "Welcome to Las Vegas" sign was designed by Betty Willis of the Western Neon Company and has been in place just south of Russell Road since 1959. On the back, it reads "Drive Carefully" and "Come Back Soon." It was added to the National Registry of Historic Places on May 1, 2009.

to Las Vegas to expand gambling operations. On December 26, 1946, Bugsy opened the 40-acre, $6 million Flamingo Hotel & Casino, the most ambitious project on the Strip yet and the oldest remaining today. With 105 rooms, a health club, gymnasiums, steam rooms, racket courts, stables, a nine-hole golf course, and upscale shopping, the Flamingo's luxury facilities easily eclipsed the other hotels in town. But what made it truly groundbreaking was the psychology behind its design: to access any area of the hotel, from guest rooms to the golf course, guests were required to walk the casino floor. Once there, the absence of daylight and clocks kept gamblers oblivious to the passage of time, while they relaxed in comfortable seating around the custom curved-edge gambling tables. The casino's massive air-conditioning units were another innovation, and made the outside world's desert heat seem distinctly unattractive. Las Vegas had a new prototype.

The Flamingo was the brainchild of *Hollywood Reporter* publisher and Black Tuesday victim William Wilkerson. A compulsive gambler, Wilkerson had played the stock market on October 29, 1929, with his $20,000 life savings and a borrowed $25,000; he was left without a dime. Within a year, Wilkerson moved to Los Angeles and published the first issue of his daily scandal sheet, to the horror of studio executives. He became a powerful figure in Hollywood, opening a series of businesses with backroom gambling on the Sunset Strip. From rags, Vendome Wine & Spirits Co., Cafe Trocadero, Ciro's, and LaRue restored Wilkerson's riches and allowed him to pursue his ambitions in Las Vegas.

Wilkerson hired architect George Vernon Russell and decorator Tom Douglas to implement his vision of a European-style hotel, in stark contrast to its Frontier-style predecessors. The Flamingo's glassy exterior, long horizontal lines, smooth curved walls, and strong geometric shape paid homage to Wilkerson's beloved Sunset Strip, but its scale and elegance were beyond his means. Just as gambling debts, dwindling funds, and soaring costs threatened to derail the entire project, Wilkerson crossed paths with Siegel and made the second-worst bet of his life by accepting a $1 million investment from the mobster and partners' business front man, G. Harry Rothberg.

At the time of its opening, the Flamingo was incomplete and short by millions, a reality concealed by a glittering entertainment lineup that included popular comedian Jimmy Durante and a host of Hollywood actors. The hotel lost

By 1968, the Strip was home to a new generation of developments such as the Riviera, its first high-rise; the Desert Inn, location for the seminal 1960s movie Ocean's 11; and Caesars Palace, the biggest, most ostentatious of them all.

Jay Sarno, former owner of the Cabana Hotel chain, opened Caesars Palace opposite the Flamingo in 1966. The 34-acre, 700-room casino cost a record-breaking $19 million, and opened with a $1 million, three-day party. Kirk Kerkorian owned the land, which he leased to Caesars before selling in 1968.

Jay Sarno's last resort on the Strip, Circus Circus, opened on October 18, 1968, and debuted on a live broadcast of the popular Ed Sullivan Show. A family twist on the traditional hotel-casino format, its pink and white big top featured trapeze artists, clowns, acrobats, and games, as well as a live elephant. MGM acquired Circus Circus in 2005 as part of its $7.9 billion merger with the Mandalay Resort Group.

$300,000 in its first week and closed two weeks later, to reopen as The Fabulous Flamingo the following March. Siegel pushed Wilkerson aside shortly after and was killed in a suspected hit by his crime partners on June 20, 1947. His murder remains unsolved.

On Labor Day 1948, the Thunderbird hotel and casino became the fourth to open on the Strip, and the second gambling venture of Marion Hicks, owner since 1941 of the El Cortez downtown. Situated across from the El Rancho, it was a return to the Strip's earlier Southwestern themes, with an earthen palette throughout, "weeping mortar" on the exterior, plus the ubiquitous use of native stone and heavy wood trusses. It featured "Wigwam" and "Navajo" rooms, and the cocktail lounge was decorated with murals of cowboys, chuck wagons, and cacti. The name itself was Navajo derived: "The Sacred Bearer of Happiness Unlimited." Though the Thunderbird was a stylistic departure from the Flamingo, Wilkerson's influence was visible in its central three-story section raised above the two-story wings and the giant neon bird sign. The Thunderbird was consistently booked from the beginning, and added the 110-room Algiers building in 1952 to accommodate overflow guests.

Rumors abounded in the press that the Thunderbird was substantially funded by organized-crime figures Jake and Meyer Lansky, and George Saldo, and in 1955 the Nevada Tax Commission responded by suspending its license. The Thunderbird was permitted to remain operational while the case was heard, and the Nevada Supreme Court later ruled in the Thunderbird's favor, revoking the suspension and clearing Hicks of all charges.

If the 1940s saw mobsters arrive, the 1950s saw them get comfortable. Resort building continued unabated, financed in large part by the American National Insurance Company (ANIC) and the Central States Pension Fund—controlled by Teamsters Union leader Jimmy Hoffa—as well as a number of moneymen with links to organized crime. Free-flowing cash meant bigger, more ostentatious developments, including the Strip's first high-rise, the Riviera, as well as the Desert Inn, the Sahara, the Royal Nevada, the Dunes, the Hacienda, Tropicana, and Stardust.

The fifth resort on the Strip, the Desert Inn, or "D.I.," opened on April 24, 1950, and became the backdrop for much Las Vegas' legend making over the next half century. Designed by New York architect Jac Lessman and built at a

Construction began on the first MGM Grand Hotel and Casino (now Bally's) in 1972. On opening day, December 5, 1973, it was one of the largest, most expensive hotels in the world, with 2,084 rooms and an initial price tag of $106 million.

Kirk Kerkorian stands in front of the construction site for the 1,512-room International Hotel in 1968. That year, Kerkorian sold Trans America Airlines to Transamerica Corporation to underwrite the project.

cost of $3.5 million, its "Crystal Showroom" hosted every major entertainment figure associated with the city, from Dean Martin and Frank Sinatra to Tony Bennett and Barry Manilow, and it was the location for the 1960s heist movie *Ocean's 11*. The Desert Inn had 225 rooms upon opening, but expanded to 325 with the addition of the St. Andrews Tower two years later. In a familiar story, owner Wilbur Clark ran short of funds during construction and turned to the mobster Moe Dalitz, whose Cleveland crime syndicate had ties to the ANIC. Clark and Dalitz's relationship did not follow the trajectory of William Wilkerson and Bugsy Siegel's, however, as Clark remained the figurehead of his resort for the entirety of his involvement, with Dalitz behind the scenes. In 1966 businessman Howard Hughes rented the entire top two floors for ten days, before purchasing the hotel from Clark for a reported $13 million.

Though the Strip had its share of luxury hotels by the 1960s, nothing forecast the opulence and scale of Jay Sarno's Caesars Palace, which opened across from the Flamingo in 1966 and changed the game. Sarno, owner of the Cabana Hotel chain, began planning the 34-acre, 700-room superdevelopment following a trip to Europe, and hired architect Melvin Grossman to create a luxurious Greco-Roman wonderland, filled with Italian Carrara marble, Classical statues, friezes, and columns, and surrounded by fountains. The hotel cost a record-breaking $19 million and opened with a three-day, $1 million party at which guests were greeted by actors dressed as Caesar and Cleopatra.

Sarno purchased the land from financier and former aviator Kirk Kerkorian, and his partners in the development included a former classmate, Stanley Mallin, and friend Nathan Jacobsen. His funding sources were less wholesome, however. Jimmy Hoffa was a former associate of Sarno's and provided a $10.5 million loan from the pension fund for the Teamsters Union. Whispers that Meyer Lansky and Chicago mobster Sam Giancana were silent investors led the State Gaming Control Board to persistently investigate Sarno, yet he opened another venture, Circus Circus, on October 18, 1968.

Located across from the Riviera and Thunderbird hotels, Circus Circus was a casino with a twist. Housed within a pink and white big top, it came complete with trapeze artists, clowns, acrobats, and games, and for a time, a live elephant. This new combination of gambling and entertainment was designed to attract vacationing families and made its debut on a live broadcast of the *Ed Sullivan*

1. Construction began in 1991 on the second MGM Grand Hotel and Casino, by which time Kirk Kerkorian had sold the original to Bally's Entertainment for $594 million.

2. Behind its shimmering green façade, MGM Grand contained 5,005 rooms, an amusement park, a 171,500-sq.-ft. casino, 12 theme restaurants, a 1,700-seat production showroom, a 630-seat theater, 3 swimming pools, live tennis courts, and an events arena.

3. Designed by Veldon Simpson, with Martin Stern, Jr., as consulting architect, the Wizard of Oz–themed MGM Grand was set to surpass its predecessor in every way. The scale of the newly constructed lion entrance hinted at things to come.

At 112 acres, MGM Grand entered 1994 as the largest hotel resort in the world.

MGM Grand opened on the Strip on December 18, 1993, at a final cost of $1 billion. Watched by Kirk Kerkorian, 5,005 green balloons, each containing a gift certificate, floated up into the Las Vegas sky as the last pane of glass was placed.

Show. Not everyone approved of the concept, however, and as Nevada law did not permit children on the casino floor, they were relegated to watching the show from a second-floor circular midway.

Circus Circus did not make the revenues Sarno anticipated, but he had hit upon a good idea—destination resorts. The next generation of hotel-casinos pushed to be much more than the sum of their parts, positioning themselves as one-stop destinations that catered to every member of the family. Circus Circus added a 400-room 15-story hotel tower in 1972, but the era truly began with the International Hotel, which opened on Paradise Road in 1969. And it was Kerkorian, not Sarno, who led the charge: Amid investigations by the IRS and the Organized Crime Task Force, Sarno resigned as operator of Circus Circus in 1969 and divested his holdings in Caesars Palace. He continued to finance Circus Circus through a series of Teamsters Union loans, but opened no new resorts.

Kirk Kerkorian was a new breed of businessman in Las Vegas, one who could secure funding from commercial banks, rather than the criminal underworld, and provide equity from his own corporations. In 1968 he sold Trans America Airlines to Transamerica Corporation and underwrote the 1,512-room International Hotel with the returns. During construction, Kerkorian's International Leisure Corporation purchased the Flamingo nearby and hired Sahara Hotels vice president Alex Shoofey as president. The Flamingo was used to train future staff for the International, but it was successful under Shoofey in its own right, showing profits of approximately $3 million in its first year.

The International's star-studded opening year saw appearances by Barbra Streisand, the musical *Hair*, and Ike and Tina Turner, as well as 58 consecutive sold-out shows by Elvis Presley. Kerkorian purchased MGM Studios that same year but suffered big losses in 1970, when loan payments forced him to sell half his shares in International Leisure to Hilton Hotel Corporation. Valued at $180 million six months earlier, Kerkorian's stock sold for $16.5 million; a relatively paltry sum, it was enough to see the International renamed the Las Vegas Hilton in 1971.

Undeterred, Kerkorian immediately began planning a new resort inspired by his recent acquisition of MGM. The first MGM Grand Hotel and Casino opened on December 5, 1973, as one of the largest, most expensive hotels in the world. Designed by Martin Stern, Jr., architect of the International, it cost a whopping

$106 million, and had 2,084 rooms, restaurants, shopping, and live jai alai for betting. The MGM Grand's two large theaters, the Ziegfeld and the Celebrity Room, quickly became popular entertainment destinations on the Strip, and the former boasted the largest stage and backstage area in the world. Donn Arden's $3 million tribute to Old Hollywood musicals, *Hallelujah Hollywood!*, ran at the Ziegfeld Room until 1980 and featured magicians Siegfried and Roy and an African lion.

Tragedy struck shortly after 7 a.m. on November 21, 1980, when a fire broke out inside the MGM Grand's Deli restaurant. It quickly spread to the second-floor

The second MGM Grand has undergone extensive remodeling since opening its doors in 1993. In 2000 the façade was revised to remove most references to the Wizard of Oz and reflect instead an Art Deco, classic Hollywood theme. And in 2011 a "Grand Renovation" saw all rooms and suites in the main hotel tower, the casino floor, and the public areas renovated and modernized.

casino and adjacent restaurants, sending poisonous gases through the hotel's air-circulation system. A helicopter rescue effort saved more than 1,000 people from the roof, but 87 were killed and 650 injured in one of the worst hotel fires in modern history. The tragedy led to greater awareness of the dangers of smoke inhalation, as most deaths occurred on the upper floors and stairwells, far from the flames. Just 90 days later, a fire broke out at the Las Vegas Hilton, leading to a major review of safety guidelines and fire codes.

Following repairs and upgrades, Kerkorian sold the MGM Grand to Bally's Entertainment for $594 million in 1986 but retained the rights to the MGM name. He opened the second MGM Grand on December 18, 1993, a $1 billion, 112-acre resort, hotel, casino, and theme park that was the largest in the world. Designed by Veldon Simpson, with Martin Stern, Jr., as consulting architect, the emerald green, Wizard of Oz–themed development surpassed its former namesake in every measurable way, with 5,005 rooms, the centerpiece 33-acre Grand Adventures amusement park, a 171,500-sq.-ft. casino, 12 theme restaurants, a 1,700-seat production showroom, a 630-seat theater, 3 swimming pools, and tennis courts, plus an arena for concerts and sporting events. At the opening ceremony, 5,005 green balloons, each containing a gift certificate, were released into the Las Vegas sky, and the final pane of glass was installed.

By the 1990s, Kirk Kerkorian had competition. The $630 million, 3,044-room The Mirage Hotel and Casino had opened on November 22, 1989, upping the stakes for the next generation of resort development and signaling the arrival of Steve Wynn on the Strip. Wynn was not new to Las Vegas, having had a stake in the Frontier since the 1960s and a controlling interest in the downtown casino Golden Nugget since the 1970s. But The Mirage was the first development in which he took an active part in the design process, working with architect Joel Bergman to create a French Polynesian–themed monument to luxury, complete with genuine gold dust–tinted windows, an indoor forest, outdoor "volcano," and an unmatched level of service. Financing for The Mirage and future Wynn projects was largely provided through low-rated, high-interest "junk bonds" brokered by friend Michael Milken of the Wall Street investment firm Drexel Burnham Lambert.

Wynn's Mirage Resorts group followed up with the adjacent Treasure Island in 1993, a $450 million hotel and casino that was linked to The Mirage and fea-

MGM MIRAGE has owned and operated the Mirage Hotel and Casino since 2000, when MGM merged with Mirage Resorts. Steve Wynn opened the $630 million, 3,044-room Polynesian-themed hotel and casino on November 22, 1989, and set a new standard for luxury with genuine gold dust–tinted windows, an indoor forest, an outdoor "volcano," and exceptional service.

tured the first permanent Cirque du Soleil show in Las Vegas. But it was the Bellagio hotel and casino, which opened on October 15, 1998, that assured Wynn's legacy as Las Vegas' premier purveyor of high-end elegance. Designed by Atlandia Design and built on what was once the site of the Dunes, Bellagio was inspired by Lake Como, Italy, and marked its departure from contemporary "themed" Las Vegas with an 8-acre man-made lake between the hotel and the Strip. The original 36-story, 3,015-room tower cost $1.6 billion, and opened with a multi-million-dollar VIP ceremony that showcased the now world-famous Fountains of Bellagio synchronized water show, as well as the hotel's gallery of fine art, and conservatory and botanical gardens.

Las Vegas, which began as a dusty road on the way to somewhere else, celebrated its centennial on May 15, 2005, as home to the largest AAA Five Diamond hotel and resort complex in the world—The Venetian, Sands Expo Convention Center, and The Palazzo. It was a proud moment for a city built by, and for, entrepreneurs and dreamers, but nothing stands still in Las Vegas. Plans were already under way for a new development that would dwarf them all and continue the city's tradition of betting big.

Steve Wynn opened the Bellagio hotel and casino on October 15, 1998, with an $8 million VIP ceremony and the world's first glimpse of the now world-famous Fountains of Bellagio synchronized water show. Inspired by Lake Cuomo, Italy, the $1.6 billion resort showcased fine art art and boasted a conservatory and botanical gardens. Bellagio became the property of MGM MIRAGE in 2000 and has since undergone $70 million in guest room upgrades.

Chapter 2

MGM RESORTS' EVOLUTION

MGM Grand began the new millennium with a period of unprecedented growth, driven by chairman and CEO Terrence Lanni, president and CFO James Murren, and director and majority shareholder Kirk Kerkorian. Lanni, a longtime senior executive in the gaming industry, joined MGM Grand in 1995 after eighteen years at Caesars World. He was joined three years later by Murren, who left his position as hotel-gaming industry analyst and Director of U.S. Equity Research at Deutsche Bank in New York City to serve as CFO at MGM Grand. Murren's team primed MGM Grand for expansion by strengthening relationships with previous and prospective banks, and briefing their associates across the U.S., Europe, Asia, and the Middle East on the company's plans for the coming decade. MGM Grand acquired Las Vegas' Primadonna Resort & Casino in 1998, and Murren became company president in 1999.

At the time Murren joined MGM Grand, Kirk Kerkorian was eighty-one years old but still relentlessly ambitious, a trait he attributes to his childhood as a first-generation immigrant. Few success stories encapsulate the American Dream as perfectly as Kerkorian's, from the streets of downtown Fresno, California, to a permanent fixture on *Forbes* magazine's billionaire's list, with assets estimated

CityCenter, a "City within a City."

at $9 billion by 2007. "When you're a self-made man you start very early in life," he told K.J. Evans of the *Las Vegas Review-Journal* in a 1999 interview (one of few). "In my case it was at nine years old when I started bringing income into the family. You get a drive that's a little different, maybe a little stronger, than somebody who inherited."

Kerkorian was born on June 6, 1917, the youngest of Armenian-born Ahron and Lily Kerkorian's four children. Ahron was a watermelon and raisin farmer, but lost his 1,000 acres during a sharp eighteen-month recession in 1921 that saw banks foreclose on mortgages. The ensuing financial difficulties forced the Kerkorians to move more than twenty times, eventually settling in Los Angeles, where the enterprising young Kirk worked as a hotel newsboy and watermelon dealer to keep the family afloat.

The family spoke Armenian at home, so Kerkorian learned English at school and as a member of a neighborhood gang. Following one too many fights, his academic career came to an abrupt end in the eighth grade, when he was sent to disciplinary school. In a pattern that would establish itself throughout his career, Kerkorian turned misfortune into opportunity, putting his street smarts to good use by training to become a boxer, coached by his older brother, Nishon. He went on to a Pacific welterweight championship, earning the moniker "Rifle Right" for his quick right hook on the boxing circuit while compiling a respectable record of 33 wins and 4 losses.

In 1939 Kerkorian accepted a ride in friend Ted O'Flaherty's small, single-engine airplane and disembarked a changed man. He funded his new, expensive passion for flying by milking cows and shoveling manure at "Happy Bottom" ranch, which was owned by celebrity female pilot Florence "Pancho" Barnes. Though eligible to join the military, Kerkorian was determined to become a licensed pilot and spent World War II flying Mosquito bombers from Labrador, Newfoundland, to a Royal Air Force base in Prestwick, Scotland. Mission RAF Air Transport Command was, in effect, a suicide mission; three out of four planes didn't make it. Kerkorian himself ran out of gas on one flight, but as the clouds parted he was close enough to glide to safety.

With the earnings from his thirty-three aircraft deliveries, at $1,000 each, Kerkorian began a small charter airline in the 1940s that transported passengers from Los Angeles to then-remote Las Vegas. Los Angeles scrap-iron dealer

Jerry Williams became a regular customer, chartering Kerkorian's plane two or three times a week. Together with Williams, Kerkorian became a fixture at the craps tables, where he regularly, and calmly, won and lost tens of thousands of dollars in an evening. "I was just overwhelmed at the level of excitement in this little town," he said in 1999. "The best times of my life were in Las Vegas." Ironically, the "father of the megaresort" has since quit gambling.

Kerkorian hit the jackpot in 1962, with what *Fortune* magazine called, "one of the most successful land speculations in Las Vegas history." For $960,000, he bought the 80-acre parcel of land opposite the Flamingo hotel on the Strip that would become the site of Caesars Palace. Kerkorian collected $4 million in rent from Jay Sarno before finally selling the land to his tenant for $5 million in 1968. That same year, Kerkorian sold his aviation business to Transamerica for $85 million in stock, and bought 82 acres on Paradise Road for his first megaresort, the International Hotel. Before the decade's end, Kerkorian had united his passion for gaming with his growing interest in Hollywood, buying stock in the struggling MGM Studios in 1969 and gaining working control of the company within the year. He went on to reorganize, sell, and repurchase MGM three times—each to his profit.

The former aviator continued to dabble as a 17 percent shareholder of Western Airlines in the 1970s and with a failed bid for Trans World Airlines in 1991. Kerkorian also expanded his business acumen to the auto industry, buying stock in the Chrysler Corporation in the 1990s and General Motors in the 2000s. Before cashing out entirely at the end of 2006, Kerkorian was GM's largest shareholder, with holdings of more than $800 million. Las Vegas, however, has always held his attention, helped in part by a professional rivalry with fellow business mogul and Las Vegas trailblazer Steve Wynn, who is twenty-four years his junior.

For Wynn, gaming was in the blood. His father, Michael, ran a bingo business on the East Coast, and Steve's first taste of Las Vegas was in 1952, at the age of ten, when his father tried but failed to obtain a gaming license in Nevada. Both returned to Utica, New York, but the younger Wynn was hooked. He returned in 1967 and purchased a small stake in the Frontier Hotel and Casino, which Wynn and his partners sold to billionaire Howard Hughes for $24 million. In the early 1970s Wynn parlayed his share of the profits from a $1 million land deal with Caesars Palace into a stake in the Golden Nugget downtown. With each resulting

In 2004, MGM MIRAGE and Turnberry Associates utilized land once occupied by the MGM Grand's theme park for the Strip's first condo-hotel, the Signature. The development's three identical Art Deco–style towers set sales records before breaking ground and ushered in a new economic model for Las Vegas.

revamp, Wynn pushed to attract a more upscale clientele to Las Vegas and laid the groundwork for his own resorts—the Mirage in 1989 and Bellagio in 1998.

Kerkorian and Wynn's twin visions for Las Vegas converged in 2000 with the $6.6 billion dollar merger between MGM Grand and Mirage Resorts. Masterminded by James Murren, the deal brought MGM MIRAGE's portfolio of resorts to fourteen, and gave the company control of more than 18,000 hotel rooms on the Strip. In Nevada, the company now owned and operated Bellagio, Mirage, New York–New York, Treasure Island, Golden Nugget Las Vegas, Whiskey Pete's, the Primm Valley Resort, Buffalo Bill's, and the Golden Nugget Laughlin, with a 50 percent interest in Monte Carlo. MGM MIRAGE also owned casinos in Detroit, Mississippi, and Darwin, Australia; two championship golf courses at the California state line; and acres of undeveloped land in Nevada, New Jersey, and Mississippi. In addition, the company managed casinos in Nelspruit, Witbank, and Johannesburg, South Africa.

Following its $7.9 billion merger with Mandalay Resort Group in April 2005, MGM MIRAGE became the largest gaming and leisure company in the world with control of 28 properties in 5 states, and more than 41,000 hotel guest rooms in 24 hotels. Among the 11 hotels it then owned on the Strip were the Mandalay Bay and THEhotel. The latter is scheduled to be renovated and renamed the Delano Las Vegas in 2013.

From the merger onward, MGM MIRAGE's lead over rival gaming companies was irrevocable. "Acquiring Mirage was the turning point for MGM," James Murren recalled in a May 2011 interview. "Obviously, we gained a lot of scale. We bought that company perfectly in 90 days from start to finish. We then cut costs and grew revenues, and it set off a series of multiple years of prosperity for MGM MIRAGE, with record years in 1999 and then 2000. Our growth was interrupted in 2001 with the tragedy of 9/11, but we recovered rapidly and had record years in 2002, 2003, 2004,

CityCenter, a "City within a City," combines residential, hospitality, entertainment, hotel, retail, casino, and recreation on an area equivalent to twelve Manhattan blocks.

2007. We had a big run. It all started with that smaller Primadonna acquisition, but the breakthrough deal was Mirage."

By 2004, Las Vegas was booming, with a record-setting 37 million visitors, $8.7 billion in gaming revenues, and soaring profits. History shows, however, that survival on the Strip requires constant innovation and creative destruction—the Dunes made way for the Bellagio, the Sands for the Venetian, the Hacienda for the Mandalay Resort Group, and many more besides. The MGM MIRAGE merger began a period of massive consolidation that saw dozens of independent companies acquired by larger brands such as Harrah's and Park Place Entertainment, which ultimately merged. While MGM MIRAGE significantly dominated the industry, its rivals had not stood still: Mandalay Resort Group's 1,000-suite THEhotel had recently opened, Steve Wynn's $2.7 billion 2,700-room Wynn Las Vegas was in the planning stages, and Sheldon Adelson had proposed a $1.8 billion, 3,000-suite addition to the Venetian casino.

As the Strip became increasingly crowded, MGM MIRAGE sought to maximize returns on the land it had accumulated through years of acquisitions. The Las Vegas economy had changed profoundly since the days when sprawling hotel-casino developments populated the highway. In 2004 land transactions reached $30 million per acre, and hotel, food, and beverage sales overtook gambling as the primary revenue stream at major casinos such as the Mirage. Analysts began to value companies based on land holdings as well as revenues, while at the same time, real-estate investors who had previously viewed the city as a purely consumer-driven investment opportunity began to see it as a hidden gem and a likely contender in the high-end residential market.

MGM MIRAGE led the charge, partnering with Turnberry Associates to become the first resort company to build a condo-hotel on the Strip. Located adjacent to MGM Grand, on what was once the hotel's theme park, Signature's Art Deco design comprised three identical towers, each with four-star luxury amenities. By the time Tower A broke ground in October 2004, it had already set a new sales record, with all 576 units sold within eight weeks. Its success, plus brisk sales at towers B and C, proved that demand for high-rise residential living was indeed growing and that a new demographic had set its sights on Las Vegas. Equally prescient were Signature's thirty-eight stories, which hinted at a new style of vertical living in the future. "Las Vegas went from a place where land was available and an inexpensive resource," said Murren in May 2011, "where buildings were built largely horizontally, in different configurations and with large horizontal parking garages to one where previous development models were just not economically feasible and certainly not attractive."

James Murren stepped outside his financial role in early 2004 to explore development ideas for MGM MIRAGE's 67-acre parcel of land between Bellagio and New York–New York. As the last significant area of undeveloped land on the Strip, with 1,200 feet of frontage on Las Vegas Boulevard, it was the prime setting for something bold and new, at a time when economic sands were shifting. Las Vegas' future as the world's premier gambling destination was far from assured. Competition from tribal casinos was growing, with revenues of $18.5 billion in 2004 against Nevada's $9.88 billion. And the loosening of regulations on gaming monopolies in 2002 had created another new competitor in Macau, China. MGM MIRAGE's operations went beyond Las Vegas, with interests in Atlantic City, New Jersey, Illinois, Michigan, and Mississippi. And while discussions were under way to form a joint venture with other gaming conglomerates in Macau, Las Vegas remained essential to the MGM MIRAGE brand.

In April 2005 MGM MIRAGE became the largest gaming and leisure company in the world following a $7.9 billion merger with Mandalay Resort Group. The deal gave MGM MIRAGE control of the north end of the Strip, 28 properties in 5 states, and more than 41,000 hotel guest rooms in 24 hotels—11 of which were on the Strip. The company was once more primed to take a new direction, one that synthesized its economic goals with a far grander aim—to create something truly awe-inspiring. "When you see great architecture, it lives forever in your memory," said Murren in May 2011, "whether it is nineteenth-century buildings in Barcelona or those dating back further, to the piazzas of Rome. Something done well, at a human scale, and with the idea of bringing people together is timeless." Project CityCenter was born.

Chapter 3

DESIGN TEAM AND MASTER PLAN

"We could have designed a new themed hotel or expanded Bellagio south or developed a stand-alone contemporary hotel-casino. It would have been interesting but predictable, and at the end of the day it would have just cannibalized our existing properties. CityCenter is none of that. It appeals to people who already come here, but it also will attract people who had heretofore no interest in Las Vegas, who are worldly, who travel to great cities, recognize superior architecture and design, seek out art galleries, museums, and public spaces that have significance." —James Murren

In early 2004 James Murren and William (Bill) Smith, president of MGM MIRAGE Design Group (MMDG), conducted a thorough analysis of the CityCenter site, brainstorming ideas for an urban development that would maximize the value of each and every square foot. Smith, a Temple University–trained architect, created 3-D perspective boards that depicted an ensemble of variously scaled residential, hospitality, entertainment, hotel, retail, casino, and recreation buildings, on an area equivalent to twelve Manhattan blocks—a "City Within a City." Murren presented his new project first to an intrigued Terry Lanni and then at

1　Left to right: Daniel Libeskind, architect; Jim Murren, CEO of MGM MIRAGE; Kirk Kerkorian, director and majority shareholder of MGM MIRAGE; and Bill Smith, president of MGM MIRAGE Design Group, attending a design meeting for Crystals retail center.

2　William Pedersen, managing principal at Kohn Pederson Fox (left), and Bobby Baldwin, president and CEO of MGM MIRAGE, attending a design meeting for the Mandarin Oriental.

3　Left to right: Sven Van Assche, vice president of MGM MIRAGE Design Group; Terry Lanni, former chairman and CEO of MGM MIRAGE; and Rafael Viñoly, principal of Rafael Viñoly Architects, attending a design meeting for the Vdara Hotel & Spa.

4　Left to right: Bill Smith, president of MGM MIRAGE Design Group; Gary Jacobs, MGM MIRAGE executive; Bobby Baldwin, president and CEO of MGM MIRAGE; and Sven Van Assche, vice president of design at MGM MIRAGE Hospitality, attending a design meeting for the Vdara Hotel & Spa.

an MGM MIRAGE board meeting, where members directed Murren and Bobby Baldwin, CEO of subsidiary Mirage Resorts, to assess the financial feasibility of "55 West," as the project was provisionally named.

With capital largely secured through MGM MIRAGE's 2005 merger with Mandalay Resort Group, CityCenter became the largest privately funded construction project in U.S. history. The company used $3.2 billion of its $7 billion unsecured credit agreement with Bank of America for the deal, leaving $3.8 billion up front, which would be offset by annual revenues of $2 billion, and a projected $2.5 billion in sales at CityCenter's residential complex. "We built three towers for the Signature condo-hotel at MGM Grand Hotel, two of which were online before CityCenter was even started," said Jim Murren in May 2004. "The first two towers were quick sellouts, and the third sold 80 percent of its inventory quickly, at around $1,100 to $1,200 per square foot." Based upon favorable numbers in Murren and Baldwin's urban planning study, the MGM MIRAGE board of directors granted final authorization to proceed with the project. However, there was one important caveat—from Kerkorian himself: "If we move ahead with CityCenter, I want it completed within five years, because I want to be around to see it." With that, he set the deadline for December 2009, just sixty months away.

With funding in place, MGM MIRAGE solicited internationally renowned architecture firms Robert A. M. Stern Architects; Ehrenkrantz, Eckstut & Kuhn Architects (EEK); and Cooper Robertson & Partners to submit conceptual master plans for CityCenter. Their remit was a new take on Las Vegas—a development that belonged on the Strip yet broke the mold of typical hotel-casino development. Each firm brought decades of expertise and a unique perspective to the task: Stern envisioned a curved pathway and buildings from Las Vegas Boulevard to Frank Sinatra Drive, while Cooper Robertson imagined CityCenter set back from the Strip by a large landscaped area, with an arched entry driveway and retail in the center. Following a six-month review process, MGM MIRAGE selected EEK's proposal for a centerpiece casino, retail, and boutique hotels along the Strip, with strong emphasis on the pedestrian experience. The firm's mixed-use planning résumé included New York City's Battery Park, as well as high-profile future developments in Canada, China, and India. And there was no more radical proposal than theirs: look to the East Coast.

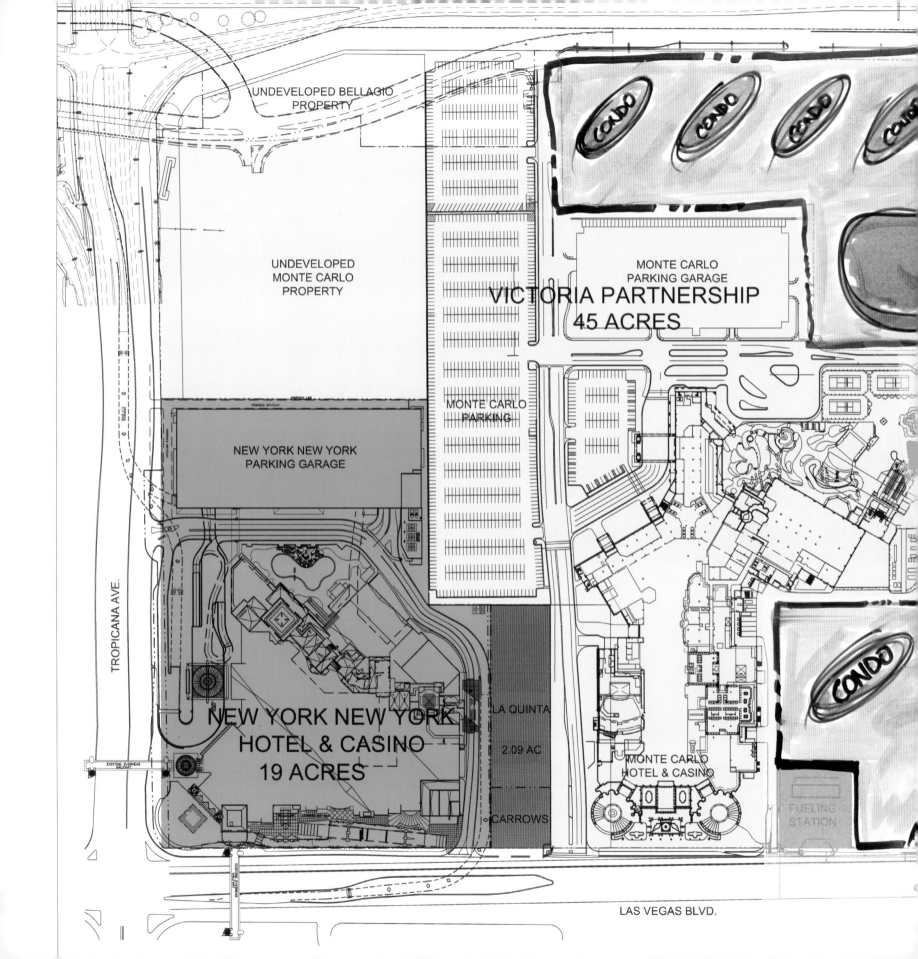

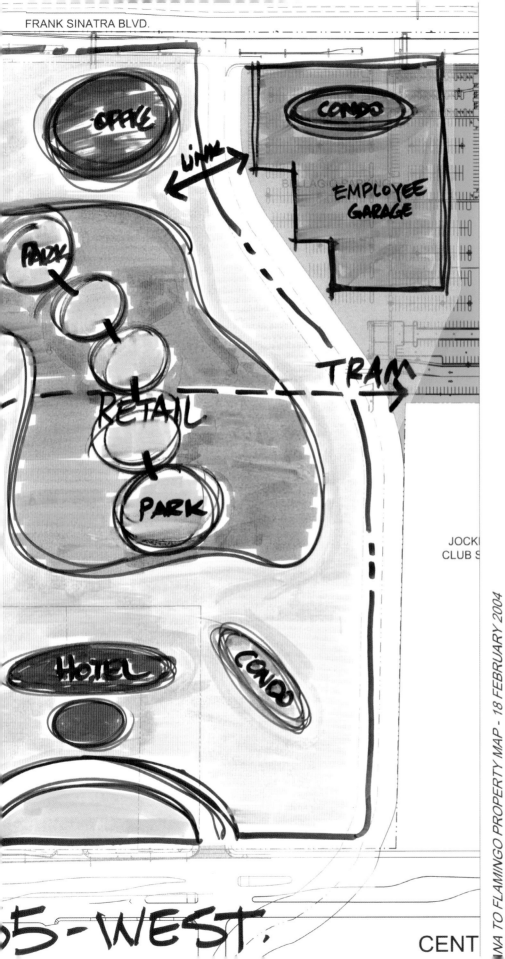

FRANK SINATRA BLVD.

OFFICE

CONDO

LINK

EMPLOYEE GARAGE

PARK

TRAM

RETAIL

PARK

JOCK
CLUB S

HOTEL

CONDO

...NA TO FLAMINGO PROPERTY MAP - 18 FEBRUARY 2004

5-WEST.

CENT

Jim Murren and Bill Smith first articulated the idea for CityCenter in a bubble diagram at a February 2004 meeting.

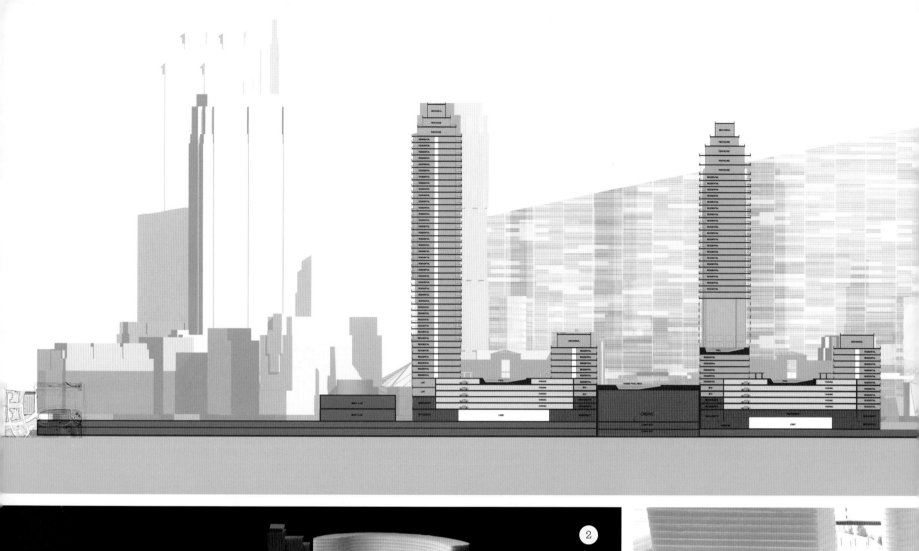

1. A proposed master plan by Robert A. M. Stern Architects illustrates residential towers with a large hotel, depicted in gray, in the background.

2. One of three master plans considered for CityCenter, Cooper Robertson & Partners' envisioned the development set back from the Strip by a large landscaped area.

3. Cooper Robertson & Partners' proposal placed an arched entry driveway and retail at the heart of CityCenter.

4. Master planners Ehrenkrantz, Eckstut & Kuhn Architects' early proposals placed retail at ground level with residential units above.

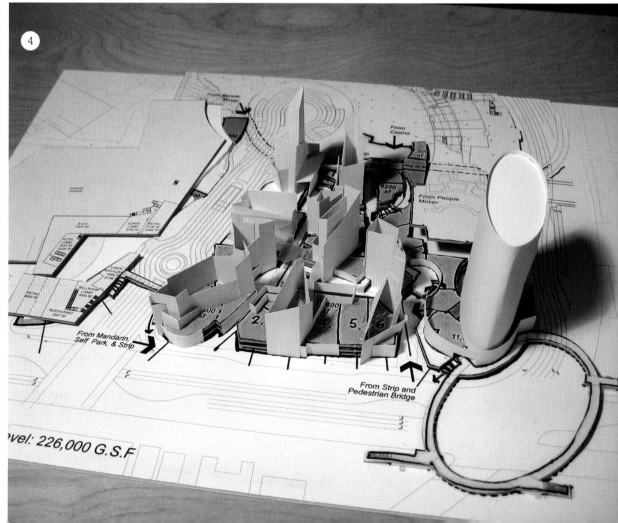

Transposed over a photograph of the Strip, Ehrenkrantz, Eckstut & Kuhn Architects' proposal for CityCenter comprised a centerpiece casino, retail, and boutique hotels. MGM MIRAGE chose the design as the basis for the development following a six-month design process.

EEK's departure point was New York City's SoHo district, an area favored by the affluent, discerning consumers CityCenter would cater to. The district's mix of mid-rise buildings, retail outlets, residences, services, and public spaces was a model of successful mixed-use development, but SoHo was greater than the sum of its parts; it was a vibrant downtown. It was SoHo's energy and density, rather than its architectural style that inspired EEK's authentically Las Vegas form of urbanism on the Strip. To illustrate the CityCenter site's raw potential, the architects transposed a scaled map of SoHo on top of its 67 acres. It was an almost perfect fit. "At that moment, I think we and the client team realized that this was no longer a casino project in the traditional sense," said Peter Cavaluzzi,

principal at EEK. "But it could have the potential to become an authentic urban place. And so that was really the launch pad for the whole project. Everything began to flow from that perspective."

The master plan placed a large, iconic hotel at the heart of the CityCenter site, around which radiated 2,400 residential units, two boutique hotels, offices, and luxury retail. To create cohesion within the diverse building program, and with the Strip, attractive walkways, underground circulation, and infrastructure were integrated from the beginning. The result is an authentic Las Vegas urban experience, yet one of a kind—by design. "From an architectural master-planning standpoint, the relationship that we were making is the kind of street environment in vibrancy and artistic atmosphere that existed in SoHo as a way to begin to think about a new city on this Strip," said Cavaluzzi. "And so we think less about quantity, we think less about specific uses or what is behind those building walls and more about the design of the environments that the buildings are creating. That's the shift of thinking that was really ground-breaking as related to development on the Las Vegas Strip."

Taking the CityCenter vision from the drawing boards to a fully realized urban development required the central oversight of an executive architect. New project president Bobby Baldwin and the MMDG team interviewed several firms during the initial planning stages and selected global architecture, design, planning, and consulting firm Gensler to partner with the in-house team to form the CityCenter design leadership team. Founded in 1965, Gensler employs more than 3,000 people in 41 locations, serving 2,000 clients at any given time. Still, CityCenter was a task of unprecedented scale and complexity, and time was of the essence. "On January 3, 2005, Bill Smith called me and told me that we had been selected as the executive architect, and we needed to hit the ground running," recalled Andy Cohen, FAIA, executive director of Gensler. "Our senior design delivery leaders arrived for work in Vegas at 8 a.m. on January 4."

Gensler assembled a fifty-person design team from twelve offices, with particular emphasis on skills such as brand strategy, development of tracking tools and databases, and guidance on sustainability, which was to be an upfront strategy. To expedite the assignment of architects, specialists, engineers, and designers for the specifics of CityCenter, the team divided the 8 million-sq.-ft. site into four distinct zones—blocks A, B, and C, plus common areas: Block A,

ARIA Resort & Casino; Block B, the Vdara Hotel & Spa, Harmon Circle, and Bellagio employee garage; Block C, the Mandarin Oriental and Harmon hotels, Veer Towers residence, and Crystals retail and entertainment; as well as associated streetscape, landscaping, and sales facilities.

After interviewing more than forty-six firms from all over the world, the leadership design team compiled a shortlist of twelve prospective project architects to participate in a seven-week intensive brainstorming session, or "charrette." Compatibility with the team at large was vital, so MMDG and Gensler met regu-

A prescient study model by Ehrenkrantz, Eckstut & Kuhn Architects shows CityCenter's retail center flanked by boutique hotels.

larly with each firm, both in Las Vegas and at their home studios. "MGM asked us to assemble a group of different architects that would be working in charrettes and design symposia and workshops," said Andy Cohen. "When they came back together again, instead of competing with each other, they were building on each others' ideas. So it was a collaboration of many, many different architects working together. That was a unique process because it allowed us to really brainstorm ideas, see what people were thinking, see the unique concepts that were coming out and build on them, versus it just being individual architects' ideas. That made a huge difference to the final product."

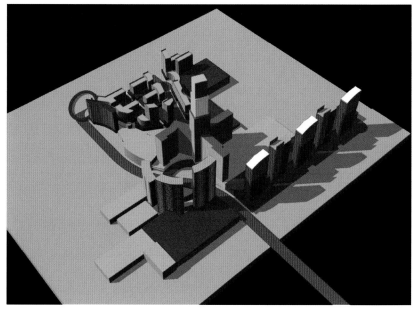

As plans for CityCenter began to take shape, Ehrenkrantz, Eckstut & Kuhn Architects produced this computer-generated model of its elements.

The leadership design team selected multinational firms Pelli Clarke Pelli for the centerpiece of CityCenter, ARIA Resort & Casino; Kohn Pedersen Fox for the Mandarin Oriental Hotel; Murphy/Jahn for Veer Towers; Rafael Viñoly Architects for the Vdara Hotel & Spa; Studio Daniel Libeskind and Rockwell Group for Crystals retail center; and Foster + Partners for the Harmon Hotel. In addition, Adamson Associates of Toronto, Canada; Leo A. Daly of Omaha, Nebraska; and HKS, Inc. of Dallas, Texas, were hired as architects of record, responsible for detailed construction drawings. Gensler and MMDG based its selections not only on each firm's fit for its individual project but also on its proven ability to work as part of an integrated whole. "One of the hardest parts was to make sure that at the end of the day, these different buildings with different atmospheres felt like integrated parts of CityCenter, not disparate parts," said Cohen. "That there would be continuity from edge to edge."

Located next to the contruction site, the CityCenter Project office building served as the main hub for the development's design leadership team.

World-class design required facilities of equal caliber. Concurrent with the search for project designers, executives from MGM MIRAGE's retail division set out to fill CityCenter's 500,000-sq.-ft. Crystals with the finest luxury brands in the world. Frank Visconti, retail president of MGM MIRAGE, and Sven Van Assche, vice president of design at MMDG, took cues from international shopping meccas such as Los Angeles' Rodeo Drive, New York City's Madison Avenue, Paris's Champs-Élysées, and Tokyo's Ginza. "We are going to build the finest hotels, including a Mandarin Oriental," Bobby Baldwin told them. "We are going

Exterior landscaping at Crystals' main entrance hints at the organic textures to be found inside.

to build condos that are equivalent to those in New York City and Hong Kong. You have to do the same thing at Crystals—only the finest luxury stores."

From the outset, MGM MIRAGE believed that the great opportunity of City-Center carried with it great responsibility to set a benchmark for sustainability. Conservation, "green" building, and responsible use of natural resources had yet to become ingrained in the culture of Las Vegas, where neon lights and man-made wonders made very real environmental challenges such as global warming and resource shortages seem like problems solved. The tide of public opinion was turning, however, and MGM MIRAGE saw forward-thinking, environmentally sensitive solutions as an added value and a moral imperative.

"We sell experiences, and we sell things that add to the quality of travel," said Cindy Ortega, senior vice president of Energy and Environmental Services at MGM MIRAGE, in June 2011. "And if you look at it, that is what the environmental movement is trying to achieve: to preserve and even enhance and increase the opportunities and quality of life for everyone, while at the same time using ingenuity and resource conservation to make it so that we have the system to support us. For MGM to design CityCenter and put it in the middle of Las Vegas is something we should do."

The CityCenter project was guided by the U.S. Green Building Council's (USGBC) LEED (Leadership in Energy and Environmental Design) program, which advocates for optimal energy performance, reduced water use, and improved indoor air quality. In March 2005 the leadership design team chaired an eco-charrette and assembled a 40-person team of LEED experts to collaborate with CityCenter's 700-plus consultants on green "master" specifications. The team created manuals on compliance strategies for all LEED credits, from diverting construction waste from landfill to the use of high-performance façades of low-emissivity insulating glass, sunshades, cool roofs, and locally sourced and/or recycled materials.

CityCenter became the largest LEED project in the world upon registration with the USGBC—in a climate where temperatures average above 80 degrees Fahrenheit for half the year and have been known to reach 117 degrees. By completion, its energy use was 68 percent of a development of similar size and density, saving 90 million gallons of water per year. The project achieved six LEED Gold certifications for sustainability in design, construction, and operation, with a 100 percent success rate. "We achieved every design certification point we went for," said Ortega. "We aimed to create a vibrant destination to demonstrate that a community can be both beautiful and sustainable."

Chapter 4

CONSTRUCTION
AND ENGINEERING

"Every time I look at CityCenter, and I think about what we have accomplished, I think about how in early 2009 a handful of people stuck by MGM—bankers, some other good advisors, our board of directors, some incredibly brave men and women who literally worked around the clock. And I think about how, without their collective effort, there would be no CityCenter, and we wouldn't be talking about the grand architecture, and the sustainability, and the ground-breaking design. We wouldn't be talking about anything but the tragedy of a shell of a construction site that would be a symbol of the Great Recession."
—James Murren, CEO of MGM Resorts International, May 2011

Anchoring of glass panels to the building façades was tackled overnight. With their curtain walls in place, CityCenter's towers shone brightly seven months from opening day.

When CityCenter broke ground on April 3, 2006, it was with a 42-month construction schedule, a $7 billion budget, and every confidence in both. The domestic and world economies were in the midst of a boom, indicated by a third consecutive year of growth, and Las Vegas had responded with increased visitor volume and gaming revenues. For MGM, the mid-2000s were a time to capitalize on the acquisitions of Mirage Resorts (in 2000) and Mandalay Bay (in 2005), which had resulted in cash flows in excess of $2 billion, $23 billion in

Much of the 1.2 million cubic yards of concrete at CityCenter was supplied by an on-site batch plant, which facilitated 24-hour construction. Pictured are multiple pumps installing concrete for ARIA's foundation.

assets, and a projected $2.5 billion in residential sales. The time, it seemed, was as good as any.

CityCenter's consolidated project schedule necessitated the construction of 7 integrated buildings, plus infrastructure. The project required approximately 12,800 skilled tradesmen on the Strip, where other projects were under way, including Donald Trump's Trump International Hotel, Steve Wynn's Encore, Sheldon Adelson's Palazzo, and Jeffrey Soffer's Fontainebleau.

MGM's reputation within Las Vegas as both a fair employer and strongly positioned business entity continued as it elected to retain a 100 percent unionized
labor force for the construction of CityCenter. With subcontractors and construction workers on board, MGM then submitted to Clark County the thousands
of architectural drawings required for individual building-permit applications.
These were prepared by Leo A. Daly, an architecture, planning, engineering, and
interiors firm, and architect of record for Vdara Hotel & Spa; Dallas-based HKS,

On April 3, 2006, CityCenter's labor force
began simultaneous construction on the
development's 7 buildings, plus infrastructure.
Starting with the placement of the tower mat
foundations, crews worked at a rate of one
floor per week, per tower.

1   With construction under way at ARIA, foundation work begins at the Mandarin Oriental (left) and Veer Towers (center).

2   As ARIA continues to rise, the Mandarin Oriental and Veer Towers—and the CityCenter layout—begin to take shape.

3   As ARIA, the Mandarin Oriental, and Veer Towers rise high, the Cubism-inspired angles of Crystals retail center begin to emerge.

4   Crystals' roof comprises 6 curving portions, 13 flat, sloping sections, and 16,455 unique fabricated steel elements. Its angles contrast with the towers of ARIA, Mandarin Oriental, and Veer Towers in the background.

5   ARIA, the Mandarin Oriental, and Veer Towers are enclosed, while Crystals' multifaceted, sky roof nears completion at the heart of CityCenter.

6   Six months prior to opening, ARIA, the Mandarin Oriental, Vdara, Veer Towers, and Crystals are nearly complete, with street-level podium work remaining.

one of the larger architecture firms in the United States, and architect of record for ARIA Resort & Casino; and Adamson Associates Architects, Inc., architect of record for the Mandarin Oriental Hotel & Residences, Crystals retail, and Veer Towers.

Adamson Associates with good reason describes itself as "A Partnership of Corporations." Founded in 1934, the full-service firm has served as executive architect to many acclaimed design architects, enhancing and implementing

projects such as Canary Wharf in London, the World Financial Center in New York City, the Petronas Towers in Kuala Lumpur, and the Fengtai Science and Technology Park in Beijing. It is headquartered in Toronto and has offices in New York, London, Los Angeles, and Abu Dhabi.

As architect of record for arguably the most complex of 25 of CityCenter's 67 acres, Adamson Associates provided master-plan coordination, design support, contract documentation, specifications, and site review. It also brought to

CityCenter occupies 67 acres south of the Bellagio. From left to right are the Bellagio parking garage, the Vdara Hotel & Spa, the ARIA tower and convention area, the CityCenter employee garage, and the development's central power plant.

the project previous relationships with five of CityCenter's six design architects: Pelli Clarke Pelli, Kohn Pedersen Fox, Foster + Partners, Studio Daniel Libeskind, and Murphy/Jahn. David Jansen, partner at Adamson Associates, described the firm's typical role as that of a "quiet player." "My analogy is that we are similar to a back-up band for rock stars—everyone knows the name of the rock star but few can name the band," he says. "On many projects, we are involved in almost all stages of project development. From the beginning we actually do the master plans, coordinate the infrastructure, and we have even gone to the extent where we have already started designing the building core before the selection of a design architect."

Clark County's review agencies coordinated permits for the CityCenter design leadership team. As part of the Clark County Development Agreement, MGM MIRAGE agreed to build pedestrian bridges, and to build and equip a fire station at CityCenter that would cut overall emergency response times on the Strip. The Clark County Fire Station No. 32 houses a fire engine and paramedic rescue unit, and responds to calls at CityCenter and surrounding hotels and business.

Concurrent with the towers and fire station, CityCenter's construction crew also built parking facilities for 16,700 vehicles; improvements along Las Vegas Boulevard; a pedestrian bridge over Las Vegas Boulevard and Harmon Road; a

4

1   Looking northwest on what will become CityCenter Drive, Veer Towers' sloping structural steel columns are visible to the right and ARIA is straight ahead.

2   An ironworker employed at the CityCenter site welds gusset plates at the Aria skylight.

3   Workers stencil temporary signs to identify areas by their various functions. This area will become a "specialty restaurant."

4   Street signage for CityCenter helps draw pedestrian traffic into the development.

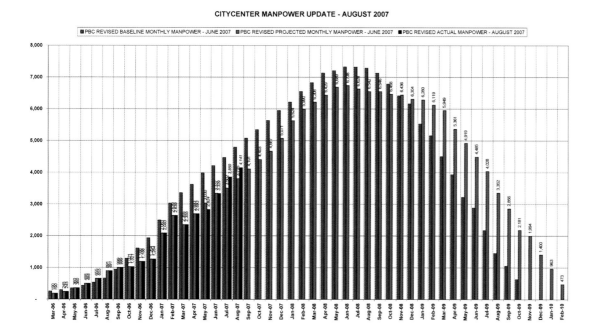

CITYCENTER MANPOWER UPDATE - AUGUST 2007

■ PBC REVISED BASELINE MONTHLY MANPOWER - JUNE 2007   ■ PBC REVISED PROJECTED MONTHLY MANPOWER - JUNE 2007   ■ PBC REVISED ACTUAL MANPOWER - AUGUST 2007

An August 2007 chart displays the projected versus the actual monthly manpower on CityCenter's construction site.

(1) Steel framing for Crystals retail center is assembled close to the base of ARIA. The "gateway to CityCenter," it faces the Strip and accommodates one of three stations for CityCenter's automated people mover.

(2) Crystals' roof comprises 6 curving portions, 13 flat, sloping sections, and 16,455 unique fabricated steel elements. Its angles contrast with the towers of ARIA, Mandarin Oriental, and Veer Towers in the background.

(3) At the base of Veer Towers, Crystals' complex structure of 6 arcade and 13 planar roofs, which connect at multiple angles to converge at its peak, was among the most challenging elements to construct at CityCenter.

(4) Crystals is accessible by tram from the Bellagio and Monte Carlo hotels and by bridge from the Mandarin Oriental, and it is physically linked to ARIA.

(5) Iron workers frame structural steel for Crystals' main entrance, which today adjoins one of the largest Louis Vuitton stores in North America.

(6) Structural steel traces the jagged outlines of Crystals' main entrance, soon to be finished in glittering stainless steel.

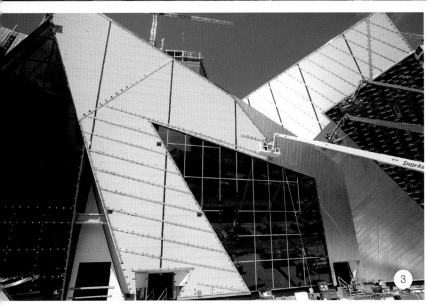

1. Construction crews work on interior drywall framing at Crystals retail center. The building's connection to Veer Towers created seismic challenges on the interior, requiring an 8-in. movement joint from the roof to street level. In the event of an earthquake, Crystals' roof and the towers would move independently of each other.

2. As Crystals' angular roof takes shape, framing for the exterior walls is just visible underneath. By opening day, sections of the roof will extend to the ground, seemingly forming part of the façade.

3. Sub-framing encloses an exterior wall at Crystals retail center in preparation for the metal and crystalline façade.

4. With the installation of its stainless-steel panels, Crystals' exterior wall begins to shimmer.

5. Crystals' roof ridge skylights flood the center's park-like interior with daylight.

6. Glass is installed in a corner store at Crystals now occupied by Gucci.

7. Workers install the final layer of Crystals' roof membrane, which reflects sunlight to naturally control the interior temperature and reduce dependency on air conditioning.

8. Crystals earned an FSC (Forest Stewardship Council) award for its use of sustainable woods, such as the reclaimed-wood flooring laid prior to opening.

9. Horizontal lighting is installed at Crystals' "treehouse." Designed by Rockwell Group, the 80-ft.-tall sculpture is now home to seafood restaurant Mastro's Ocean Club.

Of the unitized glass curtain walls that enclose CityCenter's towers, ARIA's is the largest at 1.2 million sq. ft. Its 9,600 panels were fabricated off-site and anchored to the façade over 24 months, adding considerable environmental benefits and the building's signature shimmer.

transportation system between CityCenter and the adjacent Bellagio and Monte Carlo hotels; and an 8.5-megawatt co-generation power plant. Coordinating this construction, to the specifications of hundreds of designers, required several layers of oversight, from the MGM board, through a leadership management committee chaired by CityCenter CEO Bobby Baldwin, to an execution team led by MMDG president William Smith, down to hundreds of on-site managers from MMDG, Gensler, Perini, and Tishman.

From the outset, CityCenter incurred an approximate 4–5 percent increase in construction costs to meet LEED Gold standards for energy use, waste dis-

posal, and recycling. Approximately 94 percent of construction and demolition debris was diverted from landfill; this included 124,000 tons from the old Boardwalk Hotel and adjacent structures, which were imploded to clear the site, pulverized, and used as backfill. To every possible degree, contractors reduced fuel consumption by hiring locally and sourcing regional materials such as Nevada stone. And for the health and well-being of guests, workers sealed ventilation systems and pipes during construction to prevent the infiltration of dirt and pollutants into the building interiors. Measures such as these saved energy and

At peak construction, the CityCenter site heaved with thirty-two tower cranes, scores of trucks, hundreds of four-wheel people carriers, and up to 12,000 workers daily.

water use by 30 percent, and set a sustainable precedent for CityCenter as a whole.

Retaining multiple contractors allowed each to focus on a clearly defined role. "It was more like urban construction that you would see in New York or Chicago or maybe San Francisco than you would normally see in Las Vegas," says Daniel McQuade, chief executive of construction services at Tishman. "A lot of it was the things you do in big cities—like staggering work hours, so you don't have everyone trying to get to work at the same moment in nighttime deliveries. It is a little different in Las Vegas because you have issues with heat and other things, but we used big urban project–type techniques."

Soil conditions in Las Vegas Valley can pose significant engineering chal-

1 Construction begins on one of ARIA's two multistory, steel-framed podiums, on the east and west sides of the resort. The east is now home to the casino, parking, restaurants, and retail; the west, to the resort's multilevel parking garage, spa, and rooftop pools.

2 Large mobile cranes begin the installation of structural steel at ARIA's convention center. Two steel frames brace the center east to west (600 ft.), and four north to south (350 ft.).

3 ARIA's glass curtain wall reflects the early morning sun. In a departure from the stucco panels so prevalent in Las Vegas, CityCenter's shimmering exteriors feature integrated sunscreens.

4 Concrete is pumped onto a deck of the employee parking garage, housed in ARIA's west podium.

1

2

3

4

5

5   An intermediate
     steel member
     is installed for
     ARIA's lobby
     skylight.

1   Located close to ARIA's porte cochère, Lumia by WET Design is the first water feature to display neon colors in daylight. Pictured is the installation of the fountain's structural steel and pumps, which shoot large arcs of water that "spark" as they intersect.

2 + 3   The first letter of ARIA's marquee sign arrives. Located along I-15, it is 64 x 36 ft. and is visible from three miles south.

4   White floodlighting fins were installed around the perimeter of ARIA's roof for added nighttime illumination. Perforated shades project from the top of each floor to deflect the sun light.

5 Aria sign in its final position among the rooftop white metal fins used for night illumination.

6 Metal studs frame the entrance to ARIA's Peter Remedios–designed private gaming rooms.

7 Workers install decorative marble flooring at ARIA's high-limit gaming area.

8 ARIA's private gaming rooms are gilded with gold leaf.

1. Vdara's fifty-seven-story tower is clad in alternating bands of reflective glass and acid-etched spandrel glass. The curved façade references the ARIA and the contours of the roadway below.

2. Service functions and traffic for the Vdara are accommodated on the ground floor, beneath the tower.

3. To the right, the installation of Veer Towers' curtain wall gets under way.

4. The installation of Vdara's curtain wall, which lends the building exterior its signature black and silver appearance.

lenges. Depth to bedrock in the valley varies from between several hundred feet to one mile, and the area is characterized by deposits formed by a Pleistocene lake that existed approximately 10,000 years ago. Geological exploration at CityCenter revealed variable soil types, which, combined with the wide range of building heights and stress loads, made conventional foundation construction methods almost impossible.

One rock-like material prevalent within Las Vegas, known as "caliche," varies in thickness and density, and often has to be mechanically removed during basement excavation. At CityCenter, however, engineers designed a network of 3,226 caissons, 4 ft. in diameter and 60 to 100-ft. deep, to attach to these rock-

At dawn, after a long night of placing reinforcing steel on the site, construction workers place concrete for the next floor of the Vdara.

1   Veer Towers required foundations composed of reinforced concrete mats and drilled piles. By the time of the initial Veer pour, ARIA had begun to rise in the background.

2   Two different reinforced-concrete columns were used throughout Veer: 60 in. in diameter on the first three levels, thin and round above. Concrete formwork, which protruded from the building during construction, was removed by tower cranes.

3   Veer Towers are positioned 96 ft. apart at their bases and slope 5 degrees in opposite directions. After the initial concrete pour, the towers' sloping structural columns became very evident.

4 Workers place formwork on the first elevated floor of Veer Towers as construction of the buildings' columns begins to take place.

5 A typical column-reinforcing steel cage is set before final placement of concrete.

6 Reinforcing steel is placed for the 80-ft.-tall walls of Veer Towers' identical lobbies. Once complete, the west wall will frame a view of the nearby Mandarin Oriental.

1 The Mandarin Oriental's aluminum and glass façade approaches the top of the tower. Its lower hotel and upper residential portions are divided by the two-story Sky Lobby on the twenty-third floor.

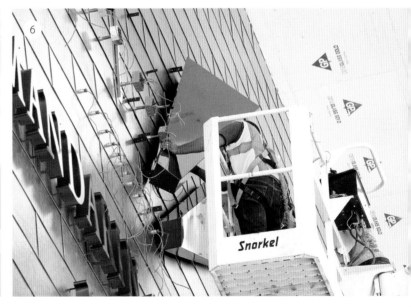

2   The first of the Mandarin Oriental's interlocking vertical aluminum panels and fritted glass are installed at the base of the tower.

3 + 4   Workers rig and then hoist an exterior wall panel for attachment to the Mandarin Oriental exterior. Each crane at CityCenter performed up to 150 lifts per working day.

5   Adam Tihany–designed wall components, in Mandarin Oriental's signature black and gold, are installed in the hotel lobby.

6   A worker affixes directional signage for the Mandarin Oriental hotel to a titanium wall.

1. Concrete columns await the completion of CityCenter's automated people mover. Designed by BergerABAM, the elevated structure connects the development's properties and CityCenter to nearby MGM MIRAGE-owned resorts.

2. Prior to carrying passengers between Crystals retail center, the Monte Carlo hotel, and the Bellagio, the 2,400-ft.-long automated people mover system was tested extensively. Today, it carries up to 3,500 passengers at 22 miles per hour.

3. CityCenter's automated people mover arrives from Doppelmayr Cable Car Ltd., headquartered in Wolfurt, Austria. Engineering and planning firm BergerABAM led the project team for its design and construction, along with guideway design.

4. CityCenter's two outdoor automated people mover stations are framed with tapered steel trusses, over which a 10,000-sq.-ft. Teflon-coated fiberglass roof will shade waiting passengers from the elements.

like deposits. Above ground, the caissons are connected by large mat foundations and grade beams, which support the structural columns upon which the towers are constructed.

CityCenter used 1.2 million cubic yards of concrete—enough for a sidewalk from Las Vegas to New York and back—most of which came from an on-site batch plant. Built by local manufacturer Rinker Materials, the plant's on-site location increased the overall quality and moisture content of the concrete in the summer heat, reduced transportation and energy costs, and facilitated around-the-clock construction. Rinker developed more than sixty mixes of varying weights and compressive strengths for floors, columns, walls, and decorative surfaces for each of CityCenter's structural-concrete buildings, which were constructed at a rate of one floor per week per tower.

The towers' shimmering appearance is thanks to their unitized curtain-wall systems, which both beautify the façades and add considerable environmental benefits. Composed of modular panels of glass and metal, each was fabricated off-site to exacting specifications to minimize assembly challenges. The largest façade, at 1.2 million sq. ft., is ARIA's, which consists of 9,600 panels of insulated glass, extruded aluminum, and stainless steel. Baker Metal manufactured the system at the firm's 200,000-sq.-ft. plant in Dallas, prior to assembly by Enclos Corporation in St. George, Utah.

Despite its size, ARIA's curtain wall posed no particular challenge for Baker Metal. "When I started in engineering, I was using a T-square, pencil and paper," says Robert Baker, founder and president. "Now the drafting and documentation is done on computers. The computer-aided manufacturing equipment in our plant fabricates the metal based on digitized designs, which reduces waste and ensures better joinery of building materials. In this way, design and manufacturing become a seamless process, cutting costs, producing superior building materials, and speeding completion of projects."

Upon arrival at the site, ARIA's 2,400-lb., two-story panels were immediately hoisted from the delivery trucks and anchored to its façade. This process was repeated approximately 9,600 times at ARIA over 24 months, and occurred mostly at night due to the high volume of activity during daylight hours. Peak construction saw 32 tower cranes, scores of trucks, hundreds of four-wheel people carriers, and up to 12,000 workers on-site daily.

One of the last remaining construction cranes at CityCenter is reflected in the Mandarin Oriental's aluminum and glass façade.

After three years of construction, however, that grand opening day almost slid out of view. CityCenter's construction was beset by a faltering economy and a wildly fluctuating commodities market, which saw its budget rise to $8.5 billion in August 2008, and the project almost ground to a halt in 2009, by which point Dubai World, the investment arm of the Dubai government, was a 50/50 investor. Dubai World's portfolio of businesses serves more than thirty countries, primarily in the fields of transport, dry docks and maritime, urban development, and investment and financial services. Its subsidiary Infinity World Development

Corp. (IWDC) came on board at CityCenter in 2007, when construction was more than 60 percent complete, with a $2.5 billion stake in the project and $1.2 billion in MGM stock.

As Dubai World's senior executive in the U.S., IWDC president William Grounds was charged with finding new buying opportunities within troubled housing markets, and gravitated toward Florida, New Mexico, Arizona, and Nevada. Having previously served as general manager at Lend Lease, developer of the 2000 Olympics, Sydney Olympic Park, and as chief executive of real-estate funds at investment group MFS Limited, Australian-born Grounds was prepared for the complexities of CityCenter. "There are many diverse aspects to the various projects that I was involved with there," he says, "so I guess it helped to work across different parts of the real-estate sphere. Here at CityCenter, we have financial issues, we have construction issues. And I think the Australian environment is probably a lot more volatile than the U.S. economy just by matter of the fact that it is a very small economy. It is easily impacted by global events, while the U.S. economy is a little more resilient. I was comfortable in that ambiguous environment."

When James Murren became chairman and CEO in early 2009, CityCenter was on the brink. "We had a bank market that refused to lend, and we had the capital markets totally frozen," he says. "And MGM MIRAGE and Dubai World were both funding a project in which we each only owned half, while our finances were deteriorating, both at MGM MIRAGE and at Dubai World." That year, Dubai World ceased additional funding for CityCenter, setting off a pivotal forty-five days of negotiations that ended with a new joint-venture agreement in a settlement and a total of $1.8 million in funding from the banks. MGM MIRAGE and its investors were then poised to complete the project and maintain CityCenter's original opening date in December 2009.

CityCenter survived, by the narrowest of margins. "If one bank, if any bank—small or large—had said no, and joined the many others that had said no, City-Center would have filed for bankruptcy, and that would have been the end of it," says James Murren. "And CityCenter would not be open today, 12,000 people would not be working, and the economy in Las Vegas, which is only now starting to recover, would be in freefall still."

Chapter 5

ARCHITECTURE AND
INTERIOR DESIGN

CityCenter's gateway from the Strip, the Mandarin Oriental, Las Vegas, and primary buildings ARIA Resort & Casino, Crystals retail and entertainment district, Veer Towers, and Vdara Hotel & Spa opened in December 2009. Each fuses a distinct architectural point of view with the philosophy of CityCenter through environmentally responsible design and the development's Fine Art Collection.

The U.S. Green Building Council for sustainable design and energy efficiency awarded five LEED Gold certifications to CityCenter, making it one of the largest sustainable developments in the world. In addition, the ARIA and Mandarin Oriental hotels received North America's most prestigious symbol of excellence in the hospitality industry—the AAA Five Diamond Award—in 2010. Bestowed upon less than 1 percent of rated venues throughout the United States, Canada, Mexico, and the Caribbean, the award is rarely given to new hotels and restaurants within their debut year.

CityCenter's Fine Art Collection is the first major permanent collection in Las Vegas to be integrated into a public space and one of the largest corporate art collections in existence. The paintings, sculptures, and installations are strategically placed in hotels and residences, along walkways, in parks, and at

The complementary forms of Vdara and ARIA rise on opposite sides of Harmon Circle and are physically linked by an elevated vehicular driveway.

intersections to elevate the experience of CityCenter visually and emotionally. Whether pre-existing pieces or singular new commissions, their awe-inspiring scale, unusual materials, powerful message, or sheer beauty enhance the surrounding architecture and the pedestrian experience.

For James Murren, it was vital that CityCenter's art and sculpture be on a par with its design and construction. "I felt that we should recruit world-class intellects from the fields of interior design and architecture and art," he said. "They could extend the boundaries of our knowledge, because they have done some tremendous works around the world. And that is exactly what happened. I think that is the magic of CityCenter: the collaboration of people whose works extend around the world, and to collectively create something that we could not have achieved at home."

Mandarin Oriental, Las Vegas

3752 LAS VEGAS BOULEVARD, SOUTH
LAS VEGAS, NV 89109

Design Architect: Kohn Pedersen Fox (KPF)
Team: Adamson Associates Architects, Architect of Record; interior design firms: Tihany Design* , Kay Lang + Associates, and Page + Steele Architects
Area: 1,100,000 sq. ft.
LEED: Gold

*Adam D. Tihany practices interior design and does not perform architectural services. References made to "architecture" relate to various aspects of interior design that may have been incorporated into the overall design scheme and indicate that he acted as a design consultant to the local architect.

The Mandarin Oriental's aluminum and glass façade glitters at sunset.

The Mandarin Oriental hotel and residential complex is both the gateway to City-Center and one of its most prominent features on the Las Vegas skyline. Located at the entrance to the development, the 47-story tower is one of few freestanding non-gaming properties on the Strip, and its gleaming aluminum and glass façade is immediately recognizable from near and far. It features 392 luxury guest rooms and suites, as well as the Residences at Mandarin Oriental—225 apartments and condominiums divided from the hotel by the 23rd-floor Sky Lobby. All guests and residents have access to the pool deck, fitness center and spa, six restaurants and bars, ballroom, and retail amenities. The hotel is the first within the Mandarin Oriental Hotel Group to achieve LEED Gold Certification.

Mandarin Oriental's distinctive fan logo is proudly displayed on the south elevation of its gleaming aluminum and glass façade.

MGM selected Hong Kong-based Mandarin Oriental Hotel Group, operator of award-winning hotels, resorts, and residences in twenty-seven countries, from a pool of thirty-six firms to operate the beacon of CityCenter. The firm's brand recognition, high-end, international customer base, and proven track record in the luxury hospitality sector was a natural fit for the hotel's prominent location, as was its relationship with project architect Kohn Pedersen Fox (KPF), designer of the Landmark Mandarin Oriental hotel in Hong Kong and the Mandarin Oriental in Macau, China.

In outlook, personnel, and practice, KPF is the definition of multinational. Since its founding in 1976 by A. Eugene Kohn, William Pedersen, and Sheldon Fox, the architecture and planning firm has grown to a staff of more than 650 that hails from 43 countries and speaks more than 30 languages. Its 23 principals and 19 directors oversee offices in 6 countries and corporate, hospitality, residential, academic, civic, transportation, and mixed-use projects all over the world. KPF's notable commissions include the Shanghai World Financial Center, Abu Dhabi International Airport, and the award-winning redevelopment of the World Bank Headquarters in Washington, D.C.

KPF's résumé of high-density urban development is exemplified by the bustling Roppongi Hills district in Tokyo, Japan, where the firm designed the majority of the buildings for developer Minoru Mori. During the selection process for the Mandarin Oriental, Bobby Baldwin, Sven Van Assche, and William Smith toured the neighborhood with KPF chairman Eugene Kohn and senior designer Ko Makabe, seeing firsthand its mix of structures of varying heights and uses, and bordering public space.

"They were interested in seeing examples of a large, urban, multi-use development, and the United States did not have that many places that we could show," says Eugene Kohn, chairman of KPF. "They could see that it was a great urban place and what modern multi-use buildings and cultural facilities can do to attract people. The art at Roppongi is very dominant. It has a great public space with a fantastic hotel, wonderful restaurants, shops, theaters, and a major office building with a school, private club, galleries, and a museum. So there were many lessons to learn from Roppongi."

The Mandarin Oriental's guest rooms and residences use a warm, neutral palette, soft, compatible textures, and natural materials.

William Pedersen, managing principal Paul Katz, and Ko Makabe led KPF's Mandarin Oriental design team, which was overseen by Eugene Kohn. "We operate as a team, rather than [as] individual celebrities," says Kohn, "so it was definitely a team project and done well." Early concepts were not focused exclusively on a single tower, but also considered two towers linked by walkways and horizontal configurations of guest rooms and residences. The final design was an angular tower clad in aluminum and glass, but KPF incorporated interesting scale and texture at the pedestrian level with a podium of granite, limestone, zinc, and titanium, and a

William Pedersen, managing design principal of Kohn Pedersen Fox, sketched this original design concept for the Mandarin Oriental.

serene bamboo garden drop-off area. Inside, the courtyard and seven-story-high atrium create a dramatic sense of arrival.

Interior designer Adam D. Tihany of New York City was a logical choice for Mandarin Oriental, having previously created luxurious, innovative spaces for MGM MIRAGE's Bellagio, Mandalay Bay, and Mandarin Oriental hotels elsewhere. Tihany Design's client base includes luxury hospitality chains Shangri-La, One & Only Resorts, and Four Seasons, as well as top-rated chefs such as Thomas Keller, Daniel Boulud, Pierre Gagnaire, Charlie Palmer, and Jean-Georges Vongerichten. Every project presents unique challenges and rewards, but Tihany particularly enjoys the no-holds-barred attitude of Las Vegas. "It is a city full of venues that constantly compete with each other for attention and need continuously to reinvent themselves to stay relevant," he says. "The visitors demand unforgettable experiences and the owners are willing to take chances with innovation and, at times, 'over the top' design."

Mandarin Oriental's eastern roots inspired Tihany's traditional Chinese-inspired color palette of black, oxblood red, and gold, against which iconic detailing, artwork, materials, and furniture are minimally distributed to evoke modern Asian cities. From the entry foyer, an elevator takes guests to the twenty-third-floor Sky Lobby, where floor-to-ceiling views of Las Vegas and a "gold bullion" wall await them at check-in. The adjacent Mandarin Bar is backlit by the Las Vegas skyline and decorated with richly patterned fabric walls and ceilings, dark wood floors, and blue mohair–covered furniture. Low-hanging light fixtures lead to the Asian-style Tea Lounge, while a glass wine loft, suspended from the ceiling, leads to Twist by Pierre Gagnaire—one of six restaurants within the hotel.

As William Pedersen explains, stepping inside the Mandarin Oriental should elicit surprise. "The Mandarin is primarily established to act as a boundary and a gateway," he says, "but it was also developed to create an inner world, and it is that inner world, I think, that makes it quite unique. It is not something that advertises itself much on the exterior, but when one goes in and finds that courtyard, or that atrium that rises up to the seventh floor—that for us is the real excitement and it something that is very carefully contained."

The Mandarin Oriental provides the first glimpse of CityCenter's Fine Art Collection with sculptures by Japanese artists Masatoshi Izumi and Jun Kaneko, an installation by Claes Oldenburg and Coosje van Bruggen, and a painting by

1. Computer-generated study models of the Mandarin Oriental explored two towers linked by walkways and horizontal configurations of guest rooms and residences.

2. A sectional model of the Mandarin Oriental shows the building's various uses and the floor that divides the hotel and residential areas (now the Sky Lobby).

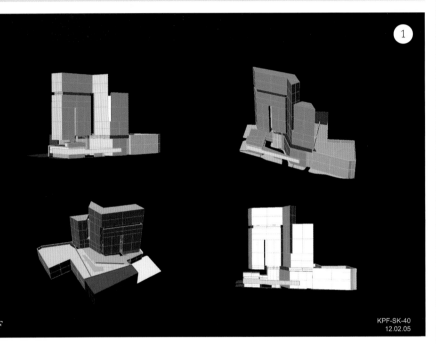

KPF-SK-40
12.02.05

3. This rendering of the Mandarin Oriental illustrates the various uses and textures at the pedestrian level. The final design incorporates a podium of granite, limestone, zinc, and titanium, and a bamboo garden drop-off area.

Adjacent to the twenty-third-floor Sky Lobby, the Mandarin Bar is backlit by the Las Vegas skyline and decorated with richly patterned fabric walls and ceilings, dark wood floors, and dark blue mohair–covered furniture.

Jack Goldstein. At 19 feet tall and weighing 4 tons, *Typewriter Eraser, Scale X*, by Oldenburg and van Bruggen depicts a giant typewriter eraser in stainless steel and fiberglass; it is located adjacent to the Mandarin Oriental at Crystals Place. Masatoshi Izumi's carved-basalt *CACTUS Life—Living with Earth* stands more than 16 feet tall at the hotel's entrance, leading to Japanese ceramic artist Jun Kaneko's three glazed monoliths in the lobby: *Untitled, Triangle Dango*; *Untitled, Dango*; and *Untitled, Dango*—the tallest of which measures 7 feet. Canadian conceptual artist Jack Goldstein's arresting acrylic-on-canvas of an erupting volcano, *Untitled (Volcano)*, hangs upstairs in the Mandarin Oriental's Tea Lounge.

Above the Sky Lobby, the Residences at Mandarin Oriental were a collaborative effort between KPF, Toronto-based Page + Steele Interior Architects, and California interior design firm Kay Lang + Associates. Luxury and penthouse units range from 1,100 to 4,000 sq. ft. and feature high ceilings, picture windows, stained-hardwood flooring, and the same sustainable features and energy-efficient Energy Star appliances found throughout the hotel. The interiors are sleek and simply detailed for an uncluttered, Zen-like atmosphere.

"We created an urban interior sanctuary, a peaceful oasis, distinctly different from all the visual stimulation and external excitement of Las Vegas," says Kay Lang, president and CEO of Kay Lang + Associates. The Los Angeles-based firm has more than thirty years experience on projects that range from the Ritz-Carlton, Key Biscayne, and the Mountain Oasis Resort, Abu Dhabi, to the Four Seasons Hotel in New York City.

At the Mandarin Oriental, Lang avoided the hard-edged hallmarks of Modernism in favor of warm neutrals, soft, compatible textures, and natural materials. Floating walls and centralized functional spaces allow for uninterrupted views and openness, while sound-absorbing materials and technology create a sense of peace and privacy. Color palettes recall both the Nevada desert and Asia, with Sovereign Jade (shades of oyster, browns, and mochas); Majestic Pearl (hues of gray and khaki); and Imperial Orchid (notes of orange and coral and light brown) predominating. Within the public areas, neutral grays and taupes set the scene for the artworks' splashes of gold, yellow, and red.

Meeting LEED Gold criteria for flooring, carpets, fabric, and fixtures, without compromising Lang's overall aesthetic, required some creative thinking on the parts of the firm and its suppliers. "When we first started the project, we wanted real zebrawood and black walnut, but given the sustainability requirements we chose engineered zebrawood instead," she says. "It was a challenge to get the look and feel of luxurious materials without using threatened species or materials produced by damaging extraction or manufacturing processes. For instance, with the bathroom vanities, we used reconstituted stone with special flecks. So we had the manufacturer create thirty samples, and selected one that had the optimal stone mixture, and looked luxurious but not too glitzy."

The twenty-third-floor Sky Lobby divides the Mandarin Oriental hotel from the residences above. Here, floor-to-ceiling views of Las Vegas and the "gold bullion" wall await guests at check-in.

A crane lowers Oldenburg and van Bruggen's *Typewriter Eraser, Scale X* into position next to the Mandarin Oriental at Crystals Place.

Oldenburg and van Bruggen's 19-ft.-tall *Typewriter Eraser, Scale X* stands adjacent to the Mandarin Oriental. The four-ton sculpture depicts a giant typewriter eraser in stainless steel and fiberglass.

A private elevator takes residents to the Mandarin Oriental's restaurants and leisure amenities, which include a 27,000-sq.-ft. spa by Tihany Design, expansive fitness center, and two lap pools. Inspired by the fashion and culture of 1930s Shanghai, the dual-level spa is one of only thirty in the world to receive the Forbes Five-Star Award and features seventeen treatment rooms, among them seven couples' suites. On the eighth-floor deck, two lap pools, shaped as long blades, reflecting the Mandarin Oriental logo, are surrounded by cabanas, two Jacuzzis, and a plunge pool.

Though KPF's role at Mandarin Oriental was highly specialized, the firm maintained open communication with MGM, interior designers, and production architects to ensure a cohesive end result. "Many architects prefer to do it all, but architects have become more specialized due to our clients' wishes to get the best experts in each area," says Eugene Kohn. "So they pick the architect for the building, an interior designer for the hotel, another for residential, and maybe another for the restaurant. We certainly had a good relationship with Adam D. Tihany and he reviewed all his designs with us, so we could relate and coordinate the interiors with the shell and core."

Due to its durable design, state-of-the-art technology and materials, and conservation policies, the Mandarin Oriental surpasses local and national energy-efficiency regulations. Meeting these key aims began with the façade, which incorporates sustainable materials, daylighting controls, reduced solar heat gain, and low emissions to account for 9 percent of the building's total energy savings. Efficient amenities and water conservation programs save an estimated 4.1 million gallons of water annually, which equates to a 45 percent reduction in potable water use. Throughout the building, nontoxic paints, sealants, adhesives, carpets, and composite-wood products reduce environmental impact, and preferred parking for alternative-fuel vehicles promotes environmentally responsible behavior within the community at large.

Setting a good example for sustainability was a primary goal of CityCenter. "I wanted sustainability to be an absolute mandatory criterion," says James Murren. "I was, and continue to be, disappointed by how little recognition is given to the fact we live in the desert. We have an almost hostile attitude toward the

The Mandarin Oriental's signature two-bedroom Dynasty suites feature an open-plan living and dining room, a working fireplace, a full study, and a marble bathroom with its own spa.

environment in Las Vegas. We have done a poor job of public transportation, of water conservation, of harnessing alternative energy, of utilizing desert plants in our commercial and residential landscapes. Instead, we have imported landscapes from around the world just to suit our own selfish taste. It is not enough for a Las Vegas resort just to put a little card in a room saying, 'If you don't want us to change the towel, hang it up and we will save a little water.'"

In addition to receiving the AAA Five Diamond Award in 2010, the Mandarin Oriental has been recognized by travel and spa guides such as Condé Nast Traveler and Spa Finder.

One of the most notable features of the Mandarin Oriental is that which is missing—a casino. Creating a luxury hotel without a gaming component in the "gambling capital of the world" was truly innovative, yet the Mandarin Oriental remains, at its core, familiar to Las Vegas. "I believe MGM decided to make a really major statement in creating a spectacular place that was more urban, very modern, high tech—a total change," says Kohn. "But I guess you can argue that, in a way, it is a theme too, in a city of themes. But we were delighted that they really wanted to create a piece of modern architecture and create a very urban place that would be quite different from any of the other projects."

As the entrance statement of CityCenter, the Mandarin Oriental has a role above and beyond its architecture program. "The ultimate measure of the Mandarin's success as a component of CityCenter is whether it stops passersby to pause and look, and whether it draws them into the complex," says Kohn. "You don't see ARIA or Vdara immediately as you come down Las Vegas Boulevard, but you do see the Mandarin."

Mandarin Oriental's eighth-floor outdoor deck features lap pools, Jacuzzis, and ultra-luxurious poolside cabanas.

ARIA Resort & Casino

3730 LAS VEGAS BOULEVARD
LAS VEGAS, NV 89158

Design Architect: Pelli Clarke Pelli Architects (PCP)
Team: HKS Architects, Architect of Record; interior design firms: Remedios Studios, Peter Marino, BBGM, Bentel & Bentel, Graft, Icrave, AvroKO, Jacques Garcia, LTL Architects, MMDG, Norwood Oliver Design Associates, RDH Interests, Richard Bloch, SLDesign, Studio A Design, Adam Tihany, Cleo Design, Richardson Sadeki, Dupoux Design, Franklin Studios, BraytonHughes Design Studios, Nakaoka / Roberts, Hamilton Anderson Associates, Gabellini Sheppard Associates, Gente de Valor, Karim Rashid, and Super Potato
Area: 6,100,000 sq. ft.
LEED: Gold

Located at the center of Casino Circle, the Lumia water feature by WET provides a fireworks-like display day and night in front of ARIA's south porte cochère.

ARIA Resort & Casino is a unifying presence at the heart of CityCenter and an awe-inspiring vision for Las Vegas and beyond. With its 600-ft.-high towers of shimmering glass and steel, it is the tallest structure on the development, from which the bright lights of the Strip are reflected back on themselves. ARIA's 4,004 guest rooms and suites are complemented by a cosmopolitan mix of 16 restaurants, 10 bars and nightclubs, and an array of luxury stores. It also features a 150,000-sq.-ft.casino, an outdoor pool, a two-level salon and spa, a convention center, and the 1,800-seat Cirque du Soleil Theater. Architecturally, ARIA is extraordinary, yet complementary, and unique to Las Vegas.

Founded in 1977, project architect Pelli Clarke Pelli Architects (PCP) is responsible for many of the most recognizable buildings in the world, from the World Financial Center in New York City to the International Finance Center in Hong Kong and the Petronas Towers in Kuala Lumpur, Malaysia. The firm brought to ARIA a long and distinguished history of sustainable architecture that began with its office tower at 30 Hudson Street in Jersey City, New Jersey—one of the first fifty buildings in the world to receive LEED certification. Most subsequent PCP projects have been LEED certified, and upon completion, ARIA became the largest LEED Gold building in the world.

As viewed from Vdara Hotel & Spa, ARIA's west side showcases the resort's counterpoising towers, glass curtain wall, and angled corners. The towers form an open center, and connect with the porte cochère and Harmon Circle.

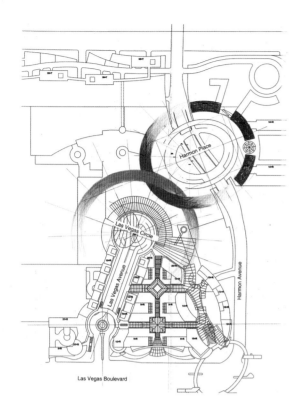

Pelli Clarke Pelli Architects' initial studies for ARIA Resort & Casino introduced curved tower shapes that would complement the early concepts for Vdara (shown upper right).

PCP developed the concept for ARIA's curvilinear, counterpoising towers during a design charrette with Kohn Pedersen Fox (KPF). While both firms explored several designs for towers, PCP's iteration of ARIA was ultimately selected for its beauty and integration with neighboring CityCenter buildings. The towers form an open center and connect with the porte cochère and Harmon Circle, while a glass curtain wall and angled corners provide panoramic views across the city and flood the interior with natural light.

As PCP hews to no single architectural style, the design process for ARIA was unusually organic, driven solely by the architects' imaginations and CityCenter's design leadership team. "This is new because the excitement in Las Vegas used to come from borrowing well-known images of famous buildings," says Cesar Pelli, founder and senior principal of PCP. "The excitement in ARIA and in the whole of CityCenter comes from the design itself, and this is a radical change in Las Vegas."

Though senior principal Fred Clarke and principal Gregg Jones led its ARIA team, PCP prides itself on the fluidity of its design process. From the firm's senior principals, principals, and associate principals to its senior associates, associates, and office staff, the firm maintains an intimate work environment in each of its studios, to the benefit of all. "We have a very organic process," says Fred Clarke. "We don't really define people's rules too terribly specifically. We are a design-driven firm, so design ideas really come from many corridors, from the most experienced to the youngest people in the office."

ARIA was a tight collaboration between architect and client. PCP captured the vibrancy of Las Vegas and expressed it in modern terms, but was guided by MGM MIRAGE's thorough knowledge of the market and the direction it was taking. The typical Las Vegas hotel model—a three-winged, Y-shaped form—had been done, and CityCenter CEO Bobby Baldwin wanted architecture unlike anything seen in the city, or any city, before. With this starting point, PCP devised two intersecting arcs, with the hotel core in the center, and rooms along every perimeter. In contrast to the boxy hotels of old, the arcs exude lightness, and provide views in every direction, as well as from all rooms.

Whereas previously, resorts in Las Vegas prompted the question, "How did they do that?" ARIA's form visibly follows function. Its façade, at once a wall of windows, a moderator of solar heat gain, and the public's first impression, lent

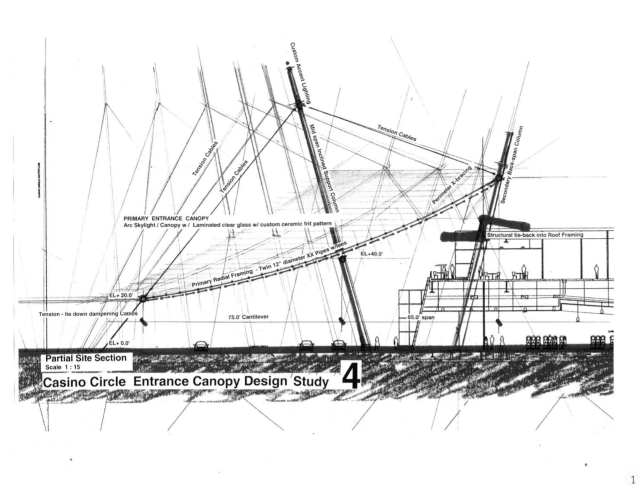

Custom Accent Lighting

Tension Cables

Mid Span Inclined Support Column

Tension Cables

Tension Cables

Tension Cables

Perimeter X-bracing

Secondary Back-span Column

PRIMARY ENTRANCE CANOPY
Arc Skylight / Canopy w/ Laminated clear glass w/ custom ceramic frit pattern

Structural tie-back into Roof Framing

Primary Radial Framing - Twin 12" diameter XX Pipes w/tees

EL +40.0'

EL+ 20.0'

Tension - tie down dampening Cables

75.0' Cantilever

65.0' span

EL+ 0.0'

Partial Site Section
Scale 1 : 15
Casino Circle Entrance Canopy Design Study 4

1. An initial design of ARIA's Cusino Circle entrance canopy details its sweeping, upward-thrusting lines.

2. Early studies of the ceiling at ARIA's front desk/registration area explored a range of materials and textures.

1

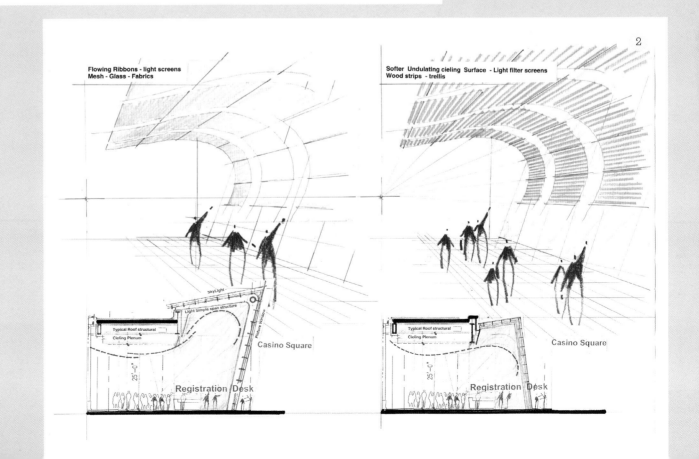

2

Flowing Ribbons - light screens
Mesh - Glass - Fabrics

Softer Undulating cieling Surface - Light filter screens
Wood strips - trellis

SkyLight

Light Simple span structure

Typical Roof structural
Cieling Plenum

Picture Window

Casino Square

Typical Roof structural
Cieling Plenum

Casino Square

25'-0"

Registration Desk

25'-0"

Registration Desk

A computer rendering of ARIA's reflective glass curtain wall illustrates its angled corners.

itself to modular construction and informs ARIA's overall aesthetic. "ARIA was a very legible building not only in the spatial sense but also in that you can see how it is built," says Gregg Jones. "If you walk around ARIA, you will see that we are very interested in how the thing was constructed. We like to express details, we like the structural systems to be powerful and very visible."

Entry to ARIA is via two "front doors"—canopied main entrances that are physically close to each other but offer contrasting first impressions. While the Harmon Circle entrance is valet only and close to nightclubs and bars, the City-Center Place arrival lobby blends natural elements such as plants, wood, and stone with contemporary art and sculpture. Under a curved, wood-beamed ceiling, it is a park-like natural setting of benches and sculptured overhead canopies; a canted glass wall behind the check-in desk provides views of a small park. The roof and vertically sloping exterior wall are entirely glazed, allowing sunlight to filter through the foliage.

In the entry lobby, Maya Lin's Silver River, an 84-ft. reclaimed-silver cast of the Colorado River, hangs on the canted glass wall behind the check-in desk, invoking CityCenter's commitment to sustainability. It may be enjoyed from the entry lobby or from the park that separates ARIA and Crystals, which also features Henry Moore's Roman travertine marble sculpture *Reclining Connected Forms*. Also in the entry lobby, three swirling, stainless-steel sculptures by Tony Cragg—*Bolt*, 2007; *Bent of Mind*, 2008; and *Untitled*, 2008—further explore the relationship between man and the built environment. Suspended within ARIA's mezzanine level is *Feeling Material XXVIII*, an 8-ft.-tall silhouette formed in steel by Antony Gormley. At ARIA's north entrance, guests are greeted by Big Edge, an installation by Nancy Rubins constructed entirely of boats.

ARIA celebrates Nevada's most precious resource with an 80,000-sq.-ft. spa complex, a 215,000-sq.-ft. pool deck, and water displays by WET, designers of the Fountains of Bellagio and The Mirage Volcano. Located within ARIA's south porte cochère are *Lumia* and

An early cross-section sketch of ARIA's 1,840-seat theater outlines the building's curved form. Today, it hosts shows by the Cirque du Soleil performance troupe.

1. Pelli Clarke Pelli created a study model of ARIA's Harmon Avenue entrance canopy—highlighting its geometry and scale.

2 Located off CityCenter Place, ARIA's elegant lobby entrance blends wood, stone, and plants with contemporary art and sculpture. Foliage canopies are lit from above to suggest sunlight peeking through the leaves. The park, an intimate garden space that separates ARIA from Crystals, is visible through the floor-to-ceiling glass curtain wall.

3 + 4 Above the front desk in ARIA's entry lobby hangs artist Maya Lin's sculpture of the Colorado River, *Silver River*. Crafted entirely from reclaimed silver, it symbolizes both the importance of water conservation and the importance of the river to Nevada as a source of energy and hydration.

1. Maya Lin's *Silver River* is installed above ARIA's front desk.

2. Artist Maya Lin describes her *Silver River* sculpture to Jim Murren, CEO of MGM MIRAGE and proponent of CityCenter's Fine Art Collection. The piece hangs above ARIA's check-in desk.

3. Bill Smith, president of MGM MIRAGE Design Group, and Jim Murren, CEO of MGM MIRAGE, discuss the installation of Henry Moore's Reclining Connected Forms in the park separating ARIA and Crystals.

4. Workers assemble the components of Henry Moore's Roman travertine marble sculpture *Reclining Connected Forms*.

5. *Reclining Connected Forms*, 1969–74, a Roman travertine marble sculpture by the late English artist Henry Moore, is located in the park that separates ARIA and Crystals. It measures approximately 10 ft. tall by 17 ft. wide and 7 ft. deep, and represents the embrace of a protective mother.

Focus: the former a reflection pool topped by sculptural fountains at the center of Casino Circle that provides a fireworks-like display day and night; the latter a 270-ft.-long curved water wall, bathed in white light, that descends a wall of gray slate tile. Within the north entrance atrium, *Latisse* comprises four separate water walls that rise 40 ft.—from the lower-level north valet to the lobby's upper-level balcony—to create a giant liquid chandelier.

Interior designer Peter Remedios, president and managing principal of Remedios Studio Inc., is a veteran of the "experience economy," having designed hotel interiors throughout the world for Aman Resorts, Hyatt International, Rafael, Regent, Shangri-La, Four Seasons, St. Regis, Westin, Sheraton, Oberoi, and Hilton. The Long Beach, California, firm based its designs for ARIA's convention center and casino on the principles of human scale that informed classical European cities, from magnetic town centers, winding streets, and intimate public spaces to the character-defining traits of neighborhoods and districts.

The 3-level, 300,000-sq.-ft. convention center includes 4 ballrooms and 38 meeting rooms, and bucks the trend for faceless, windowless corporate venues with a light-filled central atrium and a 400-ft.-long glass curtain wall on the north façade. Overlooking the outdoor pool deck, the wall connects convention-goers with the hotel's leisure facilities A 16-ft.-wide interior landscaped garden brings the outdoors in. It features more than 14,000 plants, which are visible from both sides of the glass curtain wall and elevate the building beyond mere function. "We are living in a time when design is coming into its own," says Peter Remedios. "Developers and owners are realizing the value design adds to their bottom line. In the experience economy people pay a premium for luxury products and services that are well devised and provide superior experiences."

Within ARIA, CityCenter's sole casino reverses the Las Vegas playbook by evoking the outdoors and allowing natural light to stream onto the 150,000-sq.-ft. gaming floor, which includes slots, poker, and table games. Remedios' palette of warm earth tones and foliage-like decor is in keeping with the resort's integration of natural elements and provides a relaxed atmosphere for guests, who play beneath trellis-like canopies. Vertical separations are a maximum of 5 ft. high to provide clear sightlines.

Internationally acclaimed architecture and interior design firm Peter Marino Architect designed ARIA's ground-floor high-stakes gaming areas—Salon Privé,

1. Guests arriving from ARIA's parking garage meet Tony Cragg's three swirling, stainless-steel sculptures: *Bolt*, 2007; *Bent of Mind*, 2008; and *Untitled*, 2008.

2. Located in ARIA's self-park entry lobby, Tony Cragg's stainless-steel sculptures explore the relationship between man and the built environment.

Sculptor Antony Gormley's 8-ft.-tall steel silhouette *Feeling Material XXVIII* is suspended within ARIA's mezzanine level.

Carta Privada, Radiance, and SPIN—as well as the luxurious Sky Villa, Presidential, and Entourage suites on floors 58 and 59. Each high-stakes gaming area features gilded, textured-plaster walls, a dedicated casino cage, private restrooms, and dining areas. Each Sky Villa has a living room, dining area, kitchen, exercise room, and hair salon, as well as bar and butler service. As designer of luxury flagship boutiques for Christian Dior, Chanel, Fendi, Louis Vuitton, and Ermenegildo Zegna, as well as high-end cultural and residential commissions,

Nancy Rubins' *Big Edge* sculpture is located at Vdara's main driveway and is visible from ARIA's north entrance. Composed of 200 full-sized aluminum canoes, rowboats, and flat-bottomed boats, it is a larger version of Rubins' previous work *Big Pleasure Point* at New York City's Lincoln Center.

At night, the ARIA hotel tower, south porte cochère, and Lumia water display are lit to create a dramatic effect on Casino Circle.

Conceptual artist Jenny Holzer's LED installation *Vegas* is located at the valet pickup area by ARIA's north entrance. The 280 x 18-ft. wall displays more than 200 programmed statements, including "If you live simply there is nothing to worry about" and "It's important to stay clean on all levels."

ARIA's 3-level convention center features 300,000 sq. ft. of technologically advanced meeting and convention space, with 4 large ballrooms.

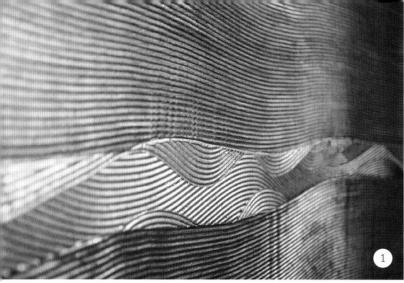

1. Peter Marino Architects specified gilded, textured-plaster walls for each of the VIP gaming rooms located within The Salon Privé.

2. Metal playing cards are a column design element in ARIA's Poker Room.

3. ARIA's high-limit gaming rooms—Carta Privada, SPIN, and Salon Privé—are accessed via private elevators designed by Peter Marino.

Peter Marino brought unrivaled understanding of the target clientele and how to wow them.

The international interior design firm of Brennan Beer Gorman Monk (BBGM) designed the exclusive one- and two-bedroom ARIA Sky Suites and Penthouses on floors 25 to 57. The suites are accessed via private elevators and equipped with advanced technology for a truly customized stay: Guests can program room preferences for lighting, temperature, audio/television systems, and draperies, and combine them to design their own wake-up experience.

The combination of services, architecture, sustainability, and art at ARIA sets the tone for CityCenter at large. "Our MGM friends are very cognizant of the fact that movements throughout Las Vegas aren't simple, they are very complex,"

Designed by Peter Marino, the exclusive Sky Villas are located in ARIA's South Tower, where the floor-to-ceiling windows provide unparalleled views of the city.

says Fred Clarke. "And the ability for these properties to intercommunicate on a multiplicity of levels and many different locations interested them a great deal."

ARIA achieved LEED Gold certification for its hotel tower, convention center, and theater, and is approximately 30 percent more energy efficient than comparable resorts. The building's principal energy saver is its glass curtain wall, which utilizes a revolutionary glass coating that filters the heat-producing rays from the sun. Guest rooms are abundantly daylit from floor-to-ceiling panoramic windows and have reduced dependence on mechanical cooling systems. Water-conservation features in all rooms and suites contribute to 31 million gallons saved each year—40 percent within the building and 60 percent in the surrounding landscaping.

According to Cindy Ortega, senior vice president of Energy and Environmental Services at MGM MIRAGE, sustainability at ARIA is more than the integration of new technology; it is an inherent philosophy. "If you walk into ARIA today, you see that the focal point above the front desk is a sculpture by Maya Lin. It is a representation of the Colorado River, because of the importance of water and the historical influence of silver in our state," she says. "And you look out, and there is a stone that was locally harvested, so we didn't have to transport it; you also have reused barn wood right there. There is also a displacement air-ventilation system that is completely unique and delivers air in a way that is cleaner and more energy efficient. That is the sustainability story, and that is the way in which sustainability is the heartbeat of this project."

Within its first year of operation, ARIA achieved the coveted AAA Five Diamond award for excellence, and the 5 Green Keys designation for sustainable operations from the Green Key Eco-Rating Program. ARIA was recognized with a second AAA Five Diamond award, for the Sky Suites, the following year.

As a cutting-edge architectural achievement and destination resort, ARIA's impact on Las Vegas has been profound. "One thing that ARIA and all of City-Center does is dispel the myth that you could only create excitement by imitating the past," says Cesar Pelli. "This shows how you can have extraordinary, exciting buildings—attractive buildings. If you are an architect, you learn much from how ARIA works, from how ARIA has been put together; how welcoming the design is to people of all ages and of all classes."

Crystals

3720 LAS VEGAS BOULEVARD
LAS VEGAS, NV 89158

Design Architect: Studio Daniel Libeskind
Team: Adamson Associates Architects, Architect of Record:
Rockwell Group, Interior Architect
Area: 700,000 sq. ft.
LEED: Gold

Crystals houses fifty-five of the world's top luxury retailers, over two stories and 500,000 sq. ft.

Crystals retail and entertainment district is located right on Las Vegas Boulevard and provides direct pedestrian access from the Strip. The 3-story, 500,000-sq.-ft. building houses 55 of the world's top luxury retailers under its multifaceted, skylit roof, from Tiffany & Co. and Bulgari to Harry Winston and Roberto Cavalli, and protects shoppers from the sun with a glittering metal- and crystalline-clad façade. Crystals is LEED Gold accredited by the U.S. Green Building Council, and is the world's largest retail district to achieve this distinction.

Design architect Studio Daniel Libeskind (SDL) is world renowned for its award-winning, culturally significant designs, among them the Jewish Museum in Berlin, Germany; the Imperial War Museum in Manchester, England; the Denver Museum of Art in Colorado; and the original master plan for New York City's Freedom Tower. Polish-born principal and lead design architect Daniel Libeskind founded the firm in Berlin in 1989, having spent time as a poet, opera-set designer, and musician. A solo artist no longer, Libeskind has offices in New York City, Zurich, and Milan, and a staff of 120.

In keeping with Libeskind's affinities for art, philosophy, literature, music, film, and theater, SDL's designs transcend their physical programs. "It's not just an inert steel and glass work," he says. "To me a good building or a city development is more like a book. It has to tell you something—a story. It tells you something about the past, something memorable. It tells you something about the future, something you didn't know, and opens a whole new world to the visitor. And that's when the building really begins."

At Crystals, SDL collaborated with Rockwell Group to create a pedestrian experience worthy of the world's greatest cities. From several entrances on the Strip, visitors step into an environment of abundant natural light, free-flowing

1. Crystals' interior architect, Rockwell Group, created this roofless study model, which depicts the retail center's various entrances and pedestrian routes.

2. Design architect Studio Daniel Libeskind (SDL) designed Crystals' structure of six arcade and thirteen planar roofs to shimmer like its namesake. Its installation was one of the most complex projects completed at CityCenter, for which construction managers kept a building enclosure schedule to track weekly progress.

3 + 4 Daniel Libeskind designed Crystals as a "gigantic work of art from every angle," as illustrated by these early concepts for the retail center's roof spine and front elevation.

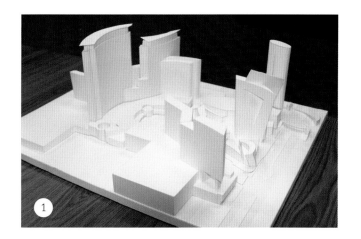

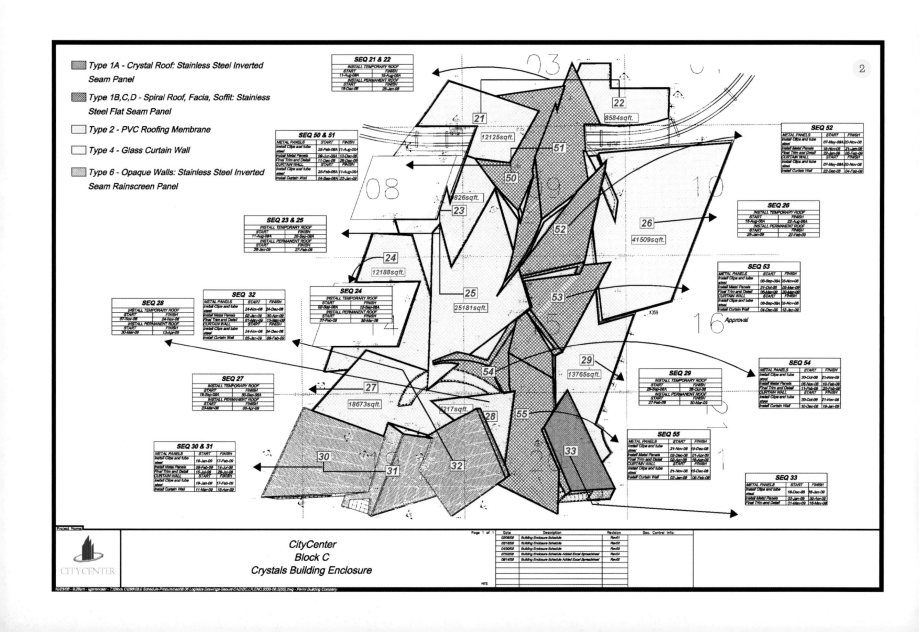

Studio Daniel Libeskind's early study model explores geometric forms for Crystals retail center's jagged roof design. The final design features no right angles.

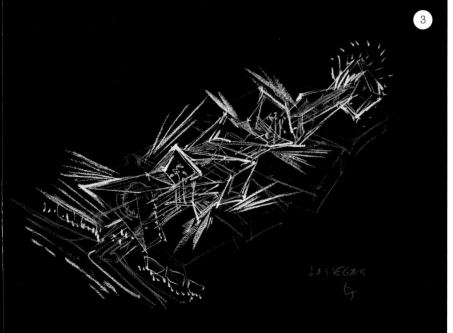

③

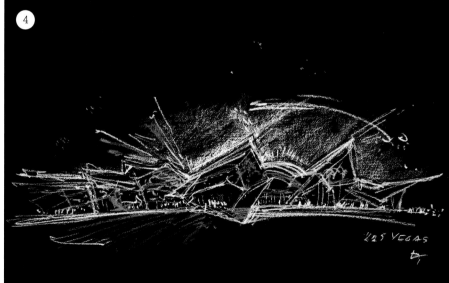

④

A study model of CityCenter's front elevation
illustrates the lines of its planar roof structure.

In an early interior design concept, Studio Daniel Libeskind imagined the contours of Crystals' multifaceted roof as seen from inside the building.

This rendering of Crystals imagines the retail center bustling with evening shoppers, some perhaps en route to the Cirque du Soleil show.

circulation, and surprises around every corner. The building is topped by a complex structure of thirteen angular roof areas, which connect at multiple angles to converge at its peak. At street level, meandering walkways interspersed with fountains, cafés, gardens, and sculpture combine retail with landscape and culture, and recall enclosed gallerias such as the Burlington Arcade in London (1819), the Passazh in St. Petersburg (1848), and Galleria Vittorio Emanuele II in Milan (1877).

"The 'wow' is not just a picture postcard; it is the continual experience that you have when you are conversing with family and friends, just walking, and just enjoying yourself," says Libeskind. "And what we are creating is something

Studio Daniel Libeskind's rendering of Crystals
along the Strip shows the retail center's
relationship to its CityCenter neighbors.

really exciting—large-scale urban space, spiraling space, that creates a land-scape within which you find the fantastic flagship stores, the fountains, and all the amenities, but also something that takes you on an urban voyage. And you really discover the complexity of the city, and the fun and pleasures that a city experience gives you."

Founded in New York City in 1984, Rockwell Group has transformed interiors such as the historic Ames Hotel in Boston, Hollywood's Kodak Theater (renamed Dolby Theater), home of the Academy Awards, and New York City's Lincoln Center, as well as numerous Broadway sets and high-end restaurants. The firm, which has a satellite office in Madrid, utilizes a variety of media, from new technology and special-effects lighting to tra-ditional fine craftsmanship and everyday materials, to express each narrative. "The single idea that we are interested in at the Rockwell Group is spaces that engage people emotion-ally," says David Rockwell, founder and CEO. "And that can be an object; that can be a huge project; it can be a show. But I'm really interested in this idea that design engages people more fully in their environment."

Crystals' interior balances SDL's sleek Modernist façade with organic textures, curved forms, and vibrant color. Striking counterpoints include a sapele-and-mahog-any sculpture that rises from the first to third floor; a 24-ft. bamboo staircase inspired by Rome's Spanish Steps; floor-to-ceiling plantings; and foliage-covered trellises. An island of seasonal flowers inspired by the biennial flower carpet at the Grand-Place, Brussels, guides pedestrians through the main thor-oughfare to a central discharge point before the casino. "We are really designing the experience from the ground up," says David Rockwell. "And by that I mean each entrance is not going to try to out-dazzle the 'city of lights' with more neon or more electric information. It is built on real materials, and on the notion of a landscape or a park growing out of the ground."

Two water features by WET, creators of the Fountains of Bellagio and The Mirage Volcano, blend seamlessly with the Rockwell Group's concept of "changeable artwork." *Glacia* produces constant, unpredictable shapes as sculp-

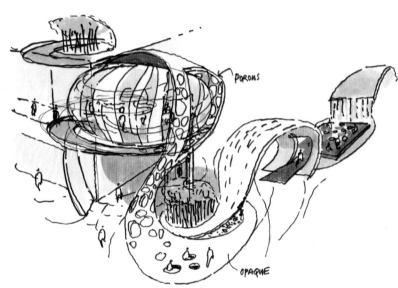

An early study by Rockwell Group outlines ideas for Crystals' "treehouse" structure. The final design retained the curved dining terrace—now Mastro's Ocean Club—and is constructed of mahogany and sapele.

tural towers of ice rise from a pool of water, while at *Halo*, clear, cylindrical water vortices materialize from the floor. "We are trying to take our cues from spectacles around the world," says Rockwell. "Look at Rockefeller Center and the Christmas tree, or the ice-skating rink. Each of those pieces is temporary—it is not there forever. So we are creating a series of installations in our landscape that will change over time."

Rockwell Group designed Crystals' interior as a twenty-first-century park, where hanging gardens serve as changeable artwork.

Peter Marino, designer of high-end boutiques, used architecture, materials, fabrics, and artwork to elevate stores for Louis Vuitton, Ermenegildo Zegna, and Fendi beyond their retail functions. By day, the embossed-steel façade of Louis Vuitton's 14,000-sq.-ft., 3-story-high flagship displays the brand's iconic "LV" logo; by night, it comes alive with a dazzling light show produced by 4,000 energy-efficient LED lights. Ermenegildo Zegna's northern Italian roots and quality woven textiles inspired Marino's palette of sky blue, Alpine green stones, and intertwined stainless steel. "Luxury should be an experience," says Marino, "a unique and memorable experience."

Crystals forms the base of Veer Towers, is physically linked to the Aria Resort & Casino, and is accessible by tram from the Bellagio and Monte Carlo hotels and by bridge from the Mandarin Oriental. To ensure a harmonious visual partnership, Studio Daniel Libeskind and Rockwell Group worked closely with CityCenter's other designers, and particularly with Helmut Jahn, design architect for Veer Towers. "CityCenter is exactly what it says," says Daniel Libeskind. "It creates a new city center for Las Vegas. It is no longer just some disparate facilities, but a new urban focus that brings things together. And that is of course, in the

A construction model displays the track of the proposed automated people mover from Bellagio to Crystals retail center.

twenty-first century, very important for ecology and for sustainability—to bring things together so you have access to the myriad of functions that the buildings are built for."

Rockwell Group's natural inspirations for Crystals' interiors went beyond appearances with the use of environmentally conscious materials and techniques that met CityCenter's goals for LEED Gold certification. In addition, the International Council of Shopping Centers (ICSC) honored Crystals' commitment to sustainability with a Gold Design and Development Award in the "Innovation Design and Development of a New Project" category.

But perhaps the most sustainable feature of Crystals is its originality. "To sustain novelty, you have to build a space that is really unprecedented," says Libeskind, "a space that is not just like the galleria in Milan or elsewhere, but a space that doesn't have a front, back, or roof. Everything has been designed in this building as a gigantic sculpture and as a gigantic work of art from every angle. It changes not just with every minute but with every heartbeat. It is imbued with a spiritual quality that is endless, that is never going to be exhausted."

Night lighting highlights the angles of Crystals' stainless-steel roof. Composed of 19 overlapping and intermingling structures, it is held together by 16,455 pieces of steel elements.

Veer Towers

3752 LAS VEGAS BOULEVARD
LAS VEGAS, NV 89109

Design Architect: Murphy/Jahn Architects
Team: Adamson Associates Architects, Architect of Record;
Dianna Wong Architecture & Interior Design, Residential
Interior Designer
Area: 900,000 sq. ft.
LEED: Gold

Viewed from the Strip, Veer Towers' identical towers rise 440 ft. above the Crystals retail center.

As CityCenter's most eye-catching feature from the Strip, only exclusively residential component, and sixth building to achieve LEED Gold, Veer Towers' distinctions are many. Its two identical 37-story towers of shimmering yellow glass rise 437 ft. above the Crystals retail center at opposing 5-degree angles, and comprise a total of 670 residences, from studios to penthouses. Each is topped by an infinity-edge pool, cabanas, hot tub, sun deck, and bar, and features indoor recreational floors that house a fitness center, private media room, steam rooms, and saunas. In a nod to classic Las Vegas, the towers boast a neon LED system by French lighting designer Yann Kersalé that emits a soft glow at dusk.

Few global architecture firms match the profile or reputation of project architect Murphy/Jahn. Based in Chicago but a global operation, the firm is known for some of the largest commissions of modern times, from the Sony Center in Berlin to the European Union headquarters in Brussels, One and Two Liberty Place in Philadelphia, and Suvarnabhumi Airport in Bangkok, Thailand. Helmut Jahn, principal since 1985, coined the word "archi-neering" to describe the firm's fusion of architecture and engineering, which stretches the boundaries of perception in the tradition of Modernist titan Ludwig Mies van der Rohe.

Murphy/Jahn's initial concepts for Veer Towers were contingent on City-Center's retail space remaining unenclosed. But when concerns about heat and humidity led to an enclosed final design for the arcade, the firm was able to integrate its early idea for leaning towers with Crytals' roof design. Cantilevered floor plates extend the towers 38.5 ft. off-center, hence the name. "A lot of our buildings are about merging public and private space, and kind of blurring the boundaries that often exist. We very much argued in the first workshops for a

totally open retail space—no boundaries, no separation between the public and the private space," says Jahn. "The key to continued success in our profession is always that you learn from what you did in the past, but you come up with something new. Not new for newness' sake, but based on what you know."

Las Vegas inspired Murphy/Jahn to explore color, form, and spatial relationships that would be beyond typical urban settings such as downtown Manhattan or Chicago. The towers' parallelogram shapes were a creative response to site constrictions, but their signature 5-degree tilt and yellow-tinted glass façades were introduced early in the design process, to practical and aesthetic benefit. By moving the towers out of each other's way, the design ensures spectacular views from both, and creates a suspended back-and-forth. "Buildings are like people," says Jahn. "People interact, and when they lean, they stir emotions. We placed the two buildings beside one another, because two people together are always better than two apart."

Murphy/Jahn drafted forty-four custom plans for the towers' "European-style" studios, deluxe studios, one-, two-, and three-bedroom flats, and penthouses, which range from 500 to 3,300 sq. ft. All feature spa-style bathrooms, open living and dining areas, and floor-to-ceiling, wall-to-wall windows. The residences' spectacular views and sense of privacy inspired Los Angeles-based Dianna Wong Architecture & Interior Design's (DWA) light, airy aesthetic. The firm's recent commissions include the Beverly Hills Hotel and Bungalows, Baha Mar Casino & Hotel on Nassau, The Bahamas, the W Hotel in Washington, D.C., and Caesars Golf in Macau, China. "My favorite feature of the building is the streamlined and expansive sense of space within it," says

Veer Towers rises 440 ft. above Crystals and features a neon LED system by French lighting designer Yann Kersalé that emits a soft glow in the evening.

Atop each tower is an infinity-edge pool with panoramic views of the Las Vegas skyline, cabanas, hot tub, sundeck, and bar. Indoor recreational floors house a fitness center, private media room, steam rooms, and saunas.

A computer rendering of Veer Towers, CityCenter's only purely residential component, illustrates the infinity-edge pools atop each identical thirty-seven-story building.

Wong. "My original design intent was to maximize its openness by extending out each surface (floors, walls, ceilings) toward the panoramic vistas. In addition, our team selected or designed every element in the residences to further the ethereal sense of suspension in the sky."

DWA's interiors are metaphors for the towers, ascending from the deep hues and tones of Earthly, to the neutral finishes of Transcendent, to the white-on-white textures of Ethereal. Three distinct color palettes evoke elements of nature—blue skies, sand, and the subtly shifting spectrum of a leaf—and are complemented by natural textures such as stone, sustainable woods, and wool and silk carpets. "A Modern architectural aesthetic permeates the details," says Wong, "making walls appear to float between floor and ceiling."

1

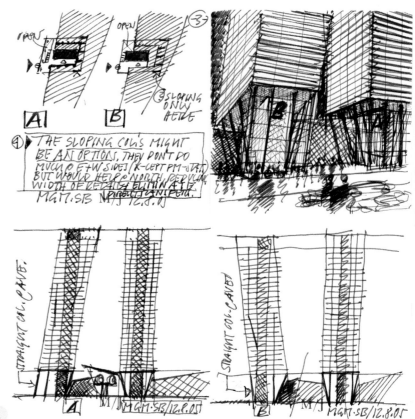

2

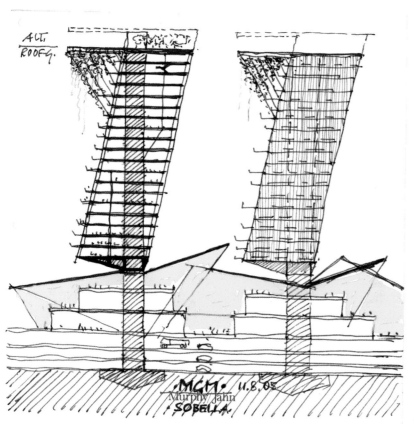

3

4

The two-level lobby provides access to Crystals, and showcases an installation by Turner Prize–winning British artist Richard Long. Against the west and east walls, *Circle of Chance* and *Earth* were formed using mud transported from the River Avon, which runs through Long's home town of Bristol. The artist hand-applied two 72- x 54-ft. images to the walls, to striking effect. Murphy/Jahn architect Francisco Gonzalez-Pulido, designer of Veer's public spaces, let Long's art take center stage, showcasing it with exposed-concrete walls and columns, and floor-to-ceiling windows.

Veer Towers earned LEED Gold certification from the U.S. Green Building Council, and uses 35 percent less energy than buildings of comparable size. Sustainability begins with the high-efficiency checkerboard curtain wall, which features 50 percent low-ultraviolet, color-fritted glass. Horizontal exterior sunshades on the east, south, and west façades divert heat for reduced energy consumption, while aluminum louvers extend 2 ft. from the building edge for additional shade. Inside, DWA utilized "eco-engineered" and recycled products such as terrazzo and bamboo flooring, faux-stone countertops, and glass tiles, and decorative lighting and plumbing fixtures that meet LEED Gold criteria for energy and water conservation, as well as low-emission paints and adhesives.

Together, Crystals and Veer Towers create a dynamic whole that expresses not only the excitement of Las Vegas, but also the modern, international outlook of CityCenter. "Until now," says Helmut Jahn, "the memory of Las Vegas' skyline was graphic; our goal was to make it architectural."

1   Veer Towers utilizes cantilevered floor plates with a 5-degree tilt—a 38.5-ft. lean from ground to roof. The towers move away from each other to ensure spectacular views from both.

2   Inspired by Las Vegas' atypical urban setting, Helmut Jahn began to explore the idea of sloped towers. Their parallelogram shape was a response to site restrictions below.

3   Initial designs for Veer Towers envisioned both buildings tilting in the same direction from Crystals' roof.

4   Early concepts explored a number of spatial relationships for the configuration of Veer Towers, as well as access routes to the buildings from Crystals' retail center.

This model of a Veer Towers residential unit showcases available finishes and color palettes.

With its exposed-concrete walls and columns and floor-to-ceiling windows, Veer's minimalist lobby was designed by Murphy/Jahn to showcase art installations by British artist Richard Long.

The towers' energy-efficient, yellow-tinted checkerboard curtain walls feature 50 percent low-ultraviolet, color-fritted glass; exterior sunshades on the east, south, and west façades, as well as aluminum louvers, provide additional shade.

Vdara Hotel & Spa

2600 W. HARMON AVENUE
LAS VEGAS, NV 89158

Design Architect: Rafael Viñoly Architects
Team: Leo A. Daly, Architect of Record; Brennan Beer Gorman
Monk, Interior Designer
Area: 1.6 million sq. ft.
LEED: Gold

Vdara's high-performance glass curtain wall shimmers in the evening. The central arc rises to fifty-five stories, while the northern and southern arcs reach fifty-three and forty-five stories, respectively.

"I think the main challenge that we face is, really, how to make a statement in Las Vegas? How do you make a statement in a city where anything goes?" Harold Park, project manager for Rafael Viñoly Architects on Block B of CityCenter (which includes Vdara Hotel & Spa, Harmon Circle, and Bellagio employee garage).

Rising opposite the ARIA on Harmon Circle, the Vdara Hotel & Spa appeals to a new generation in Las Vegas—one that welcomes proximity to the Strip, but also the option to retreat from it. The 57-story non-gaming, smoke-free condo/hotel development and spa is a sophisticated silhouette of three interlocking arcs clad in black and silver opaque glass, which responds visually to the ARIA and hugs the contours of the roadway below. A modern design program combines the energy of Las Vegas with international flair, with 1,495 units served by exclusive amenities such as a two-level wellness spa, salon, and fitness center, a pool, fine dining, and conference facilities. The Vdara is certified LEED Gold by the U.S. Green Building Council and achieved a 5 Green Keys designation from the Green Key Eco-Rating Program.

Though the original CityCenter master plan envisioned three small residential buildings around Harmon Circle, MGM MIRAGE decided that one tall, iconic building would better complement the ARIA. The design leadership team selected full-service firm Rafael Viñoly Architects (RVA) as project architect, based upon a critically acclaimed portfolio that includes the Tokyo International Forum in Japan, the Jongno Tower in Seoul, South Korea, Kimmel Center for the Performing Arts in Philadelphia, and Carrasco International Airport in Montevideo, Uruguay—Viñoly's hometown.

The Pool & Lounge Vdara is perched above the hotel's arrival porte cochère and concealed from view at ground level.

RVA was founded in 1983 and is headquartered in New York City, with offices in Los Angeles, London, and Abu Dhabi. Partner-in-charge and Vdara project director Chan-Li Lin brought twenty years of experience on large-scale international developments to the team. "My favorite part of working on a big project like this one is the interaction," he says. "Not only with those that we are directly involved with, but also with our neighboring projects—the people who design the rows that go between the projects, the people who design the automatic people movers that connect our project with other projects. To design a building not in an isolated condition, not in a vacuum, but always having to recognize and work with these other people is very, very exciting to me. So that is one of my favorite aspects of the job."

The departure point for Vdara was a single crescent-shaped slab, selected from six variations, that the architects split into three vertical slices and merged together. As a result, each floor contains six corner suites, as opposed to the usual four. A shimmering, high-performance glass curtain wall complements the ARIA's and facilitates energy conservation. "We felt that the right gesture to make from the start was to take a first step with a curved building," says Chan-Li Lin, "and somehow make that curve gesture into an interesting architectural form that has a special visual impact, not only of itself, but when it is seen together with the Pelli tower and Harmon Circle—together as a cohesive urban environment."

In the spirit of CityCenter, Vdara takes the focus upward. The tower meets its base one floor above ground level, segregating service and support traffic from public functions and creating a sense of separation. On the rooftop of the grand entrance, the 40,000-sq.-ft. Pool & Lounge Vdara is an urban oasis, overlooking CityCenter and the frenetic energy of the Strip. A large main pool, as well as private retreats, cabanas, and semi-secluded plunge pools allow guests to choose their level of engagement—or escape—among contemporary decorative elements of brushed-mahogany timbers, polished metals, and cleverly combined glass and mirrors.

There were challenges in reaching for the sky. "We have a very large pool that is elevated as much as 70 ft. off the ground," says Chan-Li Lin. "That is unusual from the standpoint of being up there where you can catch plenty of sun, but at the same time, you need to be able to effectively evacuate every-

This vertical view of Vdara highlights the three separate building setbacks.

1 Rafael Viñoly Architects' initial design for Vdara Hotel & Spa consisted of three curved, tiered blocks.

2 This early charcoal rendering of Vdara Hotel & Spa's front elevation depicts the crescent form developed by Rafael Viñoly Architects to contour to the roadway below and reference the ARIA Resort & Casino.

3 A second sketch by Rafael Viñoly Architects shows the three interlocking arcs that compose the Vdara.

4 This study model of the Vdara displays the six corners on each floor, as opposed to the usual four, that were created by slicing the tower into three.

5 Building signage at Vdara along the curved glass curtain wall.

4

5

A computer rendering of the Vdara at Harmon Circle illustrates its relation to the streetscape and ARIA (right).

Rendering of Vdara illustrating the pool deck above the porte cochére.

one in the case of an emergency. Concerns like that were big challenges, but it makes for an interesting and exciting urban environment, where things are not laid out horizontally but vertically. The overall layout of the building is very, very unusual."

Architecture and interior design firm Brennan Beer Gorman Monk (BBGM) complemented RVA's contemporary exterior with public spaces and guest

Frank Stella's 1969 work *Damascus Gate Variation 1*—an 8 x 32-ft. canvas of interlaced multicolored semicircles—hangs above the Vdara's registration desk. The lobby also features a monumental display of illuminated natural stone and a composition of suspended sculptural light sticks (foreground).

rooms that fuse desert forms, colors, and textures with urban sophistication. Founded in 1987, the firm is based in New York City, Washington, D.C., and Shanghai, China, and has broad international experience on projects ranging from small boutique hotels and luxury residences to mixed-use buildings. Its portfolio includes the Centara Grand Hotel in Bangkok, Thailand, and the Futian Shangri-La Hotel in Shenzhen, China.

The Vdara's dramatic lobby is dominated by a monumental display of illuminated local stone and a composition of suspended sculptural light sticks. Like all public spaces within Vdara, it is oriented to the south to maximize natural daylight and shadow, and take full advantage of the building's glass exteriors. American painter Frank Stella's 1969 work *Damascus Gate Variation 1*—a 32-ft. x 8-ft. canvas of interlaced multicolored semicircles—dominates the room and continues CityCenter's Fine Art Collection. Suspended over the reception desk, it is complemented by the lobby's highly textured walls of banded stone, which reference the painting's horizontality, and natural-stone flooring.

Prior to arrival in the lobby, guests are greeted by Nancy Rubins' 57-ft.-tall steel-and-aluminum sculpture *Big Edge* at the main drive. A colorful composition of aluminum rowboats, canoes, and various river and ocean vessels, connected by thousands of pounds of steel wire, it forms what Rubins describes as a "blooming flower." And nestled into the facing walls of the concierge lobby, American artist Peter Wegner's paper-and-steel installation *Day for Night, Night for Day* spans 34 x 10 ft. and 45 x 10 ft. Its components correspond with the rising and setting of the sun.

In the private realm, each of Vdara's one- and two-bedrooms, duplexes, and suites is decorated in one of three opulent and neutral color schemes, each with a unique feature color: French Chartreuse, a free-flowing combination of browns and creams, with a budding green; Royal Currant, a geometric-inspired collection of neutral textures enhanced by full-bodied Merlot notes; and Belgian Truffle, a blend of rich chocolates and creams, accented with caramelized amber.

"The design goal entailed creating a relaxed and harmonious environment infused with sophisticated urban energy," says Julia Monk, partner-in-charge at BBGM. "By alluding to the desert's timelessness, the design achieves a sense of monumental horizontality and peacefulness. Through the artful manipulation and repetition of imagery, textures, shapes, forms, bold color schemes, and lush materials, the design elements bring into focus volume and texture taking on a vast and horizontal feeling."

Inside and out, the Vdara's environmentally conscious materials and practices met the rigorous criteria for LEED Gold. BBMG's interiors utilized certified woods, low-emitting VOC paints, adhesives, coatings, sealants, and plastic laminates, as well as non-formaldehyde MDF panels and eco-friendly carpets and fabrics, while the exterior's silver and black high-performance opaque glass panels absorb sunlight to control solar heat gain and reduce heating and cooling costs. Lighting controls with energy-efficient lighting, such as T5 high-output fluorescent lamps with LEDs, reduce the power usage to 15 percent below ASHRAE (American Society of Heating, Refrigeration, and Air Conditioning Engineers) standards, and bathroom fixtures use water and energy-saving technology such as low-flow. In addition to LEED Gold, the Vdara achieved the 5 Green Keys designation from the Green Key Eco-Rating Program for its sustainable operations, and in 2011, the AAA Four Diamond Award for overall excellence. The latter applies to just 3.6 percent of AAA-approved lodgings.

Creating a cohesive element of CityCenter and a bold architectural statement in its own right was a test of RVA's collaborative skills. The result, however, is a restrained, sophisticated anchor for Harmon Circle. "We tried with our design to develop a relationship and seamless connection with Harmon Circle and CityCenter," says Rafael Viñoly. "Vdara tries to articulate the mass of a very large building into three pieces that read more like a sculptural piece in a very minimal way. I think it has an appropriate aesthetic simplicity that respects what others have done at CityCenter."

"It's really not about the cheap imagery that a lot of people associate with Las Vegas," he adds. "It is really about the intrinsic value of the quality of architecture, and urban design."

A construction worker adjusts a cable during
the installation of Nancy Rubins' *Big Edge*.
The sculpture's boats are connected by
thousands of pounds of steel wire, arranged in
a web.

Nancy Rubins' 57-ft.-tall *Big Edge* dominates
the foreground at Vdara.

1. One component of Peter Wegner's paper-and-steel installation *Day for Night, Night for Day* is hung in Vdara's concierge lobby.

2. Vdara's concierge lobby featuring the 34- x 10-ft. and 45- x 10-ft. paper-and-steel installation *Day for Night, Night for Day* on facing walls.

3. *Day for Night*, one of the two pieces in Peter Wegner's installation in Vdara's concierge lobby. Together, they represent the rising and setting of the sun.

3

Vdara's one- and two-bedrooms, duplexes, and suites are decorated in one of three color schemes, each with a unique feature color: French Chartreuse, browns and creams accented with budding green; Royal Currant, neutral textures enhanced by full-bodied Merlot notes; and Belgian Truffle, rich chocolates and creams, offset with caramelized amber.

Chapter 6

LANDSCAPE ARCHITECTURE

Of CityCenter's 67 acres, almost 16 are gardens, populated with more than 200,000 trees, shrubs, and flowers, from desert oaks, pines, and acacias to yuccas, palms, and cacti. In Las Vegas' climate of high temperatures and dry winds, these oases oxygenate and cool walkways, add color and softness to the towers of glass and steel, and create a sense of place. MGM MIRAGE retained seven firms to design CityCenter's landscapes, and invested $7.2 million on-site, plus an additional $1.2 million on new greenhouse and nursery facilities for their upkeep. The result is a living, breathing context for CityCenter that enlivens the Strip.

With its portfolio of cultural, civic, corporate, and educational commissions, the Office of James Burnett (OJB), executive landscape architect, was well versed in the challenges and goals of CityCenter. Founded in 1989, the Houston-based firm had a previous relationship with CityCenter executive architect Gensler and had recently transformed the "West Coast Camp David" Sunnylands retreat in Rancho Mirage, California, into a desert botanical garden. At CityCenter, OJB applied its knowledge of difficult climates and exacting sustainability standards to MGM MIRAGE's larger vision. "It seemed to me that one of

CityCenter's landscaping along Las Vegas Boulevard was inspired by Crystals' geometric roof design and conception as an interior park.

the overriding goals for the project was that by hiring a great design team, they would have great design," says OJB principal Jereck Boss. "This was a project that wasn't 'themed.' It was, 'What is great design? What is the future? What are the right things that are happening in design?'"

Together with MGM MIRAGE's horticulture and environmental-sustainability teams, OJB oversaw all levels of CityCenter's landscaping program and coordinated plant selection, waterproofing, and irrigation systems. While the success of native plants such as agaves might seem assured, CityCenter's "micro-climates" posed location-specific difficulties such as intense glare or magnification from the glass towers, which challenged even the hardiest of desert plants. Finding suitable replacements while considering color palettes and light requirements across the board was a matter of trial and error. "We tried to validate a lot of the plant choices by testing plantings on site to determine their performance," says Boss. "Since plants are a living, breathing, changing thing, sometimes they work, sometimes they don't. And it's not for lack of due diligence—it's just the combination of all the conditions."

CityCenter's irrigation system delivers moisture and nutrients to each plant species with minimal waste, resulting in 60 percent less water usage than landscapes at comparable Las Vegas resorts. Moisture-sensor probes trigger or shut off water, which is administered via bubblers at plant locations and drips, and supplemented by "fertigation," whereby fertilizer is injected into the water source for delivery to plant roots. "I think with the landscape architecture and with LEED and with water conservation and just being responsible with the resources that we have, there was an underlying honesty in that landscape," says Boss. "The water is a precious resource; we are going to use it sparingly, and we are going to try and balance the plant material with natives and adaptives, pushing the desert landscape a little more strongly than it has been in the past. I think those were the underlying goals that everyone was working towards together."

To control costs and increase efficiency, OJB implemented standardized construction details and installation instructions for landscape design firms Hargreaves Associates, Martha Schwartz Partners, D.I.R.T. Studio, James Corner Field Operations, Meléndrez, and J. W. Zunino & Associates. Whereas architects typically specify plant materials for purchase by the contractor, MGM MIRAGE ordered in bulk, for storage at its 21,000-sq.-ft. greenhouse and 10-acre exterior nursery at nearby Cedar Creek Golf Course. Direct procurement saved $1.4 million in markups and allowed architects and contractors to utilize a numbering system for plants and trees that sped up the installation process and minimized errors.

The process of selecting plants for the landscape architects' pool was collaborative and sparked the creativity of all involved. Teams spent two to three years visiting farms, selecting trees and plants, and looking for materials that would not only thrive in their environment but also set CityCenter apart. "We would go to California with a group of the architects, and I would work with brokers and find growers that had new and unique specimens," says Richard Honzo, director of horticulture at ARIA. "And we would go on tagging trips once a month, finding new materials. And as we went through and found unbelievable species, we would find ways to incorporate them into the landscape. Hence the changing drawings."

Local soil scientist John P. Smith developed two soil systems for CityCenter: a lightweight one for the 86 percent of plant material that is contained, and a second, more conventional blend, for on grade. Smith, a consulting horticulturist and now-retired professor of landscape horticulture at the Community College of Southern Nevada, developed the first blend to manage the critical weight allowances for planters without compromising healthy growth. The $1.1 million "super soil" combines lightweight green sand from Nevada, a composite wood blend from California, and an organic mix known as Denali Gold. "With that blend, we were able to meet our weight requirements," says Honzo. "We had amazing, organic, well-drained soil. It probably has the highest amount of organic matter and positive fungi than any other blend we could find."

While the landscape program's primary goal was to link together CityCenter's architectural elements, each landscape firm was selected for its unique point of view: Hargreaves Associates for Mandarin Oriental's ground-level arrival zone, pool roof, and pedestrian walkway; James Corner Field Operations for ARIA's open spaces and pool deck; and D.I.R.T. Studio for Las Vegas Boulevard frontage, CityCenter Boulevard, and Crystals. "We had different architects assigned to each building or block of the project, and we wanted them to give each building its own identity, to create environments that were fresh, new, and

inviting," says Richard Honzo. "At the same time, we needed that landscape to tie each of the properties together. The landscape is one of few aspects that connect CityCenter as one solid project. And that was extremely tricky—not to appear as five buildings that went up at different times, but as one project, with each area having its own identity."

Hargreaves Associates' philosophy for every project, at every scale, is connection—between culture and the environment, people and the land. Founded in 1983, the firm built its early reputation breathing life into once-derelict "dead sites," among them Kentucky's Louisville Waterfront Park and San Francisco's Crissy Field. Today the firm comprises three senior principals and seven principals, with offices in San Francisco, Cambridge, Massachusetts, New York City, and London, and is the recipient of thirty-four national landscaping awards. Recent projects include London 2012 Olympic Park, for which the firm transformed 100 hectares of neglected parklands into sweeping lawns, a promenade, public seating, and river access.

At Mandarin Oriental, Hargreaves Associates took advantage of the hotel's multiple levels to create three landscapes distinct in material and plant choices, atmosphere, and style. "One of the ideas that we abandoned early was that we were going to have some grand unification between the three spaces," says George Hargreaves, founding principal. "We treated the pool, the mezzanine, and the outer court entry as three separate spaces, because they had three functions and were in three separate locations."

The journey begins at the shaded arrival court, beneath CityCenter Place, where dark green bamboo stalks draw the eye upward against the limestone, zinc, and titanium of the hotel tower. Hargreaves Associates selected Giant Timber Bamboo (*Bambusa oldhamii*) for its ability to thrive without direct sunlight, tolerance of cold as well as heat, and subtle associations with the Mandarin Oriental brand. While this plant often reaches heights of 80 ft., it is expected to reach a still considerable 45–50 ft. to provide respite from the heat. "As you enter that courtyard, you are entering another world that is quieter," says Hargreaves. "Everything we did down there really tried to go with quietness, luxury, and a little bit of a Zen experience, which of course, goes with the Mandarin Oriental."

Eight floors up, the Mandarin Oriental pool deck maintains a sense of open-

The landscaping at Mandarin Oriental—the entrance to CityCenter—incorporates spacious sidewalks and lush greenery to draw pedestrian traffic from the Strip.

The Zen garden walkway that connects Mandarin Oriental with the Strip and ARIA features twenty-six mature black pine Bonsai trees contained in sculptural urns.

ness despite its dense program. Hargreaves Associates collaborated with hotel architects Kohn Pedersen Fox and Tihany Design to accommodate sufficient shade seating alongside the cabanas and cafés that surround the two lap pools, plunge pool, and two whirlpools. After several iterations in which the pool changed shape and was relocated, consensus was reached on a final design that positioned the main entrance on the center of the long "blade" lap pool for easy pedestrian flow, and divides the pool into an upper and lower level, linked by a natural water feature.

Though Hargreaves Associates had completed numerous hotel arrivals and promenades, the pool complex at Mandarin Oriental was its first. "We carried out our own design imprint into the project and what we wanted to do with it, but we worked with these guys who have done a lot of resort work, have done a lot of cabanas, have been through the conversation about pool deck seating," says George Hargreaves. "It was a real learning experience for us. One of the questions we are asked is, 'What is your favorite space?' Well, that is like, 'Which is your favorite child?' We love them all equally. But the pool space was new to us, new to our firm, new to me, new to Brian, so it was fascinating to us."

As the cabanas, restaurant, and café were so critical to the circulation and overall success of the pool deck, Hargreaves Associates met regularly with Tihany Design to ensure a cohesive outcome. Together, the firms devised optimal uses of space such as cabanas that could operate as two separate units one day and be collapsed into one "mega cabana" the next, and a narrative that linked architectural and landscaping features with furnishings. "Adam Tihany wanted to make sure that the pool deck had some whimsical qualities," says Brian Jencek, principal at Hargreaves Associates. "He was very interested in how narrative and poetry could weave through the space, and he translated that eventually into the idea of inscribing on the back wall of each cabana a screen of the various tree species that are located throughout the pool deck."

A 500-ft.-long walkway at CityCenter Place connects Mandarin Oriental with the Strip and neighboring ARIA. In the style of a Zen garden, lines of patterned paving direct pedestrian flow around large sculptural urns, each of which contains a black pine Bonsai tree—selected for its minimal water requirements. Though Bonsai is a time-intensive art form, it so happened that a grower in San Diego had twenty-six mature trees that needed a new, permanent home. "He had brought from Japan, as a young man, black pine seed that he later planted

The initial landscaping plan for the ARIA porte cochère depicts hardscape and plantings. At ARIA, James Corner Field Operations designed the resort's four pools, adjoining gardens and walkways, and the convention center's indoor-outdoor sloped garden.

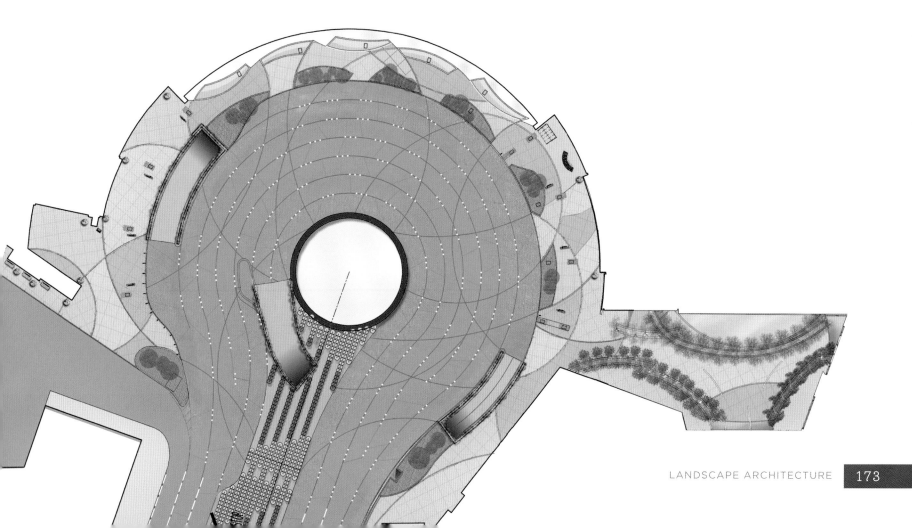

The ARIA pool deck features four elliptically shaped pools, each of which is surrounded by a unique combination of plant families, from soft grasses and textural succulents to perennials, shrubs, and trees. For ease of use, the pool deck entrance is located next to the hotel spa.

1 Designed by James Corner Field Operations, ARIA's 215,000-sq.-ft. pool deck recalls an exotic botanical garden with pools of varying depths set among planting beds, seating terraces, pathways, and fountains that soften the scale of the convention center to the left.

2 ARIA's pool deck with sculptural desert plantings for a lush environment that can withstand temperature extremes. To ensure guest safety, there are no species with needles, spines, tough leaves, poisonous berries, or staining fruits.

and trained into Bonsai trees over the next fifty years—some very large ones," says Brian Jencek. "He had one thousand, and then trimmed them down to one hundred, and what we see today is every single one of the last ones."

Through the use of natural tones and textures, Mandarin Oriental's landscapes reference both the hotel interior and the desert beyond. Hargreaves Associates drew upon red hills and mountains, and the orange hues of sunlight for a palette that is innately sustainable and speaks to CityCenter's larger goals. "We needed tones that were light enough so we wouldn't create too much heat there on the pool deck and burn people's feet," says Brian Jencek. "We also didn't want tones that were so light that they created glare, or too much reflection. So when we thought about color, it became about the sustainability, about the surrounding environment and where we are in the larger scheme of things."

For New York- and London-based James Corner Field Operations (JCFO), CityCenter was an opportunity to explore not only planting but also form, geometry, materials, furnishing, lighting, and design. The firm's holistic approach applies to commissions of all scales, from intimate gardens to large-scale urban redevelopment such as Manhattan's High Line park and Seattle's Central Waterfront. As designer of the largest area at CityCenter, the firm was responsible for ARIA's five pools plus adjoining gardens and walkways, as well as the convention center's indoor-outdoor sloped garden and additional landscaping components around Harmon Circle, the VIP drop-off area, and the site perimeter streetscape.

"MGM MIRAGE was looking to create something new and innovative, a place where contemporary design was to be foregrounded," says James Corner, founding principal. "One of the slightly unfortunate perceptions of landscaping is that it is only concerned with the planting design, and that this can occur later in the process. But in actual fact, we see landscaping as everything under the sky: everything spatial, hard, soft, structural, and open. As such, we like to be involved in any project fairly early on in order to make sure that the open space is already off to a good start structurally."

Rectangles, hard edges, and formality are notably absent from ARIA's 215,000-sq.-ft. pool deck, where desert-inspired forms and an organic sequence of pools and plantings recall an exotic botanical garden. JCFO designed the pool deck for all ages and interests, and therefore eschewed a single, large body of water in favor of three primary pools and one adult pool of varying sizes and

3 Shaded walkways provide respite from the sun and link ARIA's four pools.

4 Planting beds provide moderate shade for sunbathers on the ARIA pool deck terraces.

5 Associates from James Corner Field Operations traveled around California, Arizona, and Nevada for almost two years to select plants for ARIA's pool deck. .

6 The slope garden at ARIA's convention center features bold geometric patterns on both sides of the curtain wall. James Corner Field Operations used barrel cactus throughout, but the agave pattern is divided between *Agave attenuata* indoors and the hardier *Agave weberi* outdoors.

CityCenter's 1,200-ft. frontage on Las Vegas Boulevard was designed by D.I.R.T. Studio (Dump It Right There). A pedestrian zone was created along the building façades.

depths. Natural curvilinear forms such as sand dunes inspired concentric ellipses of planting beds, seating terraces, pathways, and fountains, all of which soften the scale of the surrounding architecture. "The large scale of the site meant that some of the inspiration came from wind-blown and water-shaped geomorphologic formations like dunes and washes, which have this very dynamic quality to them because they have been shaped over time," says Corner.

Each of the three main pool "rooms" is distinguished by a unique combination of plant families, from soft grasses and textural succulents to perennials, shrubs, and trees. At the largest, the Yucca pool, sculptural *Yucca rostrata* combines with a base planting of Leucophyllum, Blue Nolina accents (*Nolina nelsonii*), and splashes of color from change-out plants such as Purple Aeoniums and Red Kalanchoes. Large Mediterranean fan palms (*Chamaerops humilis*) provide shade at the Palm pool, accented by pockets of Mexican grass tree (*Dasylirion quadrangulatum*) and Dwarf Bottlebrush (*Callistemon citrinus*), or "Little John." And at the Acacia pool, the delicate leaves of the Willow Acacia (*Acacia salicina*) filter harsh sunlight among groups of *Yucca gloriosa*. Surrounding each of the pool areas is a ring of planting that highlights the main walkway. These enclosure species include large multi- and single-trunk date palms (*Phoenix dactylifera*), interspersed with bottle trees (*Brachychiton populneus*). A continuous ribbon of shrub understory planting—Wheeler's Dwarf (*Pittosporum tobira*)—is enlivened with green Foxtail Fern, Blue Fescue, and yellow-flowered Gazania rigens for year-round color.

JCFO associate Elizabeth Fain LaBombard spent almost two years traveling around California, Arizona, and Nevada in search of an authentic planting palette for the pool deck's extreme hot and cold temperatures. To add another layer to the challenge, concern for guest safety ruled out many species with needles, spines, tough leaves, poisonous berries, and staining fruits. "One of the really unique and wonderful things about this project is that the client really wanted fabulous specimens and allocated resources towards finding them," she says. "The plants you see most in Las Vegas are part of a very limited palette of what works in these extreme conditions. Usually, people avoid the plants that are more typical of a desert landscape and with the few staples that will create a lush and comfortable environment for the guest. Our goal was to create a desert-lush environment using many of these green staples as the base while

1 CityCenter's landscaping along Las Vegas Boulevard was inspired by Crystals' geometric roof design and conception as an interior park.

2 The planting pattern on Las Vegas Boulevard is limited to small groves that emphasize Crystals' vertical planes and ensure that the retail center's storefronts remain visible.

introducing many sculptural desert plants that are typical of the desert landscape, but not of a pool deck environment."

The convention center's slope garden presented a host of unusual conditions for JCFO, not least of which was the transition of the design from the interior to the exterior, on a sloped structural deck. Maintaining a visual connection between the bold geometric patterns on both sides of the curtain wall was critical, and required plants that looked similar yet had quite different needs. To choose them, the firm divided planting selection into three categories: interior, exterior, and both. The barrel cactus is used throughout, but the agave pattern is seamlessly divided between Agave attenuata indoors and the hardier Agave weberi outdoors. "It was a very challenging situation, made more challenging as the architects would frequently revise the design of the curtain wall," says Corner. "The challenge for us was how to create something bold, something visually arresting and distinctive. We came up with a sort of wavy pattern using gravels and a lot of differently colored and textured and succulents."

While JCFO's was the largest share of CityCenter's landscape program, D.I.R.T. Studio—"Dump It Right There"—designed its most visible components: Las Vegas Boulevard, Casino Boulevard, Casino Square, and a portion of Crystals' interior. Julie Bargmann, designer of regenerative landscapes and associate professor of Landscape Architecture at the University of Virginia's School of Architecture, founded the self-described "small and mighty" firm in 1992. Since then, D.I.R.T. has revitalized sites such as New York City's High Line, Turtle Creek Water Works in Dallas, and the Ford River Rouge Complex in Dearborn, Michigan.

CityCenter was a departure for D.I.R.T., whose work typically focuses on brownfield and derelict sites. The firm was very familiar, however, with working collaboratively, and with the parameters of working in the public realm. "I think we had one of the most fertile opportunities in the project from a landscape architecture standpoint," says Chris Fannin, former associate of D.I.R.T. Studio (now with global design firm HOK). "We had limits in terms of width and height and things like that, but the basic premise and the way in which the design problem was shaped gave us so many opportunities within it. As we investigated, we began to understand levels and space, and the ways of setting up interactions with people, buildings, heights, levels, and all these subtleties."

D.I.R.T.'s primary challenge for CityCenter's 1,200-ft. frontage on Las Vegas Boulevard was to integrate the dual functions of pedestrian zone and channel to Crystals into one cohesive whole. As Rockwell Group conceived of Crystals as an interior park, D.I.R.T. envisioned the Strip as its exterior counterpoint, linked together and to their contexts through a common design vocabulary, inspired by Libeskind's geometric roof design. "Our design language and vocabulary on Las Vegas Boulevard flows through Crystals up into Casino Square and around to Casino Boulevard," says Fannin. "We thought of the building literally moving away these flows, moving through this canyon in a set of geological formations. It was really about these big chunks, which is a pretty appropriate narrative."

To ensure that Crystals' storefronts remained visible and that pedestrian flow was not restricted, the planting pattern on Las Vegas Boulevard was limited to small groves of palms, pines, and desert oaks—each oriented to emphasize Crystals' vertical planes. CityCenter Boulevard, which extends from Las Vegas Boulevard, allowed for more flexibility in the use of color and texture. Here a blue-green Vermont slate provides chunky base materials for prickly planted forms, adding warmth and interest to an area that is almost entirely hardscape. "You have the yellow of Veer Towers and the sandstone that is the portal to the casino, and the color of the Mandarin, and the steel of Crystals," says Fannin. "So the challenge was finding something that would somehow work with these different tones, which are all very strong, but not necessarily sympathetic to one another."

As proponents of "collaborating until it hurts," D.I.R.T. Studio found CityCenter surprisingly painless. "CityCenter is a once-in-a-lifetime project," says Fannin, "given its scale, collaboration among stellar architects and artists, and total commitment to design excellence. It is quite inspirational to be part of a project that was driven by the belief that the absolute best design makes a difference both to the bottom line and to our culture."

For CityCenter's landscape team, opening day was the first opportunity to evaluate the success of planting, paving, and walkways. It became apparent that looks were not enough, as guests gravitated toward some areas and avoided others, regardless of their beauty. "We sat back and took about two hours to relax, and then we started seeing the reaction of the hotel guests and the community," says Richard Honzo, director of horticulture at ARIA. "We paid very close attention to foot traffic, how they were reacting, and how the landscape was affecting them. And though we had created some landscaped areas that were beautiful, we had actually made a few mistakes. The plants were phenomenal, but not all complemented the area and softened the landscape."

Enhancements began immediately on the structural design of agave at City-Center Place and the connecting roadway between the ARIA and Vdara. At the first, the team responded to complaints about high temperatures by adding acacia trees and desert mulch, while at the second, new planters transformed cold, uninviting concrete into a welcoming green environment. "I go there now and it is extremely elegant, very luxurious," says Honzo. "It really evokes an emotional calmness with the water features nearby. It is absolutely striking. So I think

Exterior landscaping at Crystals' main entrance hints at the organic textures to be found inside.

Crystals' storefronts illuminate the palms, pines, and desert oaks that buffer the retail center's frontage on the Strip.

we really nailed it by opening up our eyes and seeing past—not getting stuck in—our design that we had been focused on for years, paying attention to our consumers, and adjusting to their needs and demands."

From five examples of architectural innovation, the CityCenter landscape program made a single, connected urban downtown. "As the project grew, my knowledge, my opinions about horticulture and landscape improved," says Honzo. "At first, I was able to see each hotel, each block, independently and see the beauty, definition, and independence of each project. It wasn't until later on in the project that I was able to know how they worked together. CityCenter has its own style, and it is amazing that we were able to achieve that."

Chapter 7

OPENING AND OPERATIONS

On December 1, 2009, Vdara Hotel & Spa became the first building at CityCenter to open its doors to the world. Crystals retail and entertainment district followed on December 3, Mandarin Oriental on December 4, and the ARIA Resort & Casino in one final grand opening celebration on December 16. Despite many challenges, CityCenter met its sixty-month development deadline, and MGM MIRAGE's Director Kirk Kerkorian was indeed there to see the project realized. Speaking at the official opening, MGM MIRAGE Chairman and CEO Jim Murren said, "ARIA and CityCenter reflect a combination of innovation, energy, and visionary design that we believe will reshape how the world views the destination resort experience and attract visitors from around the globe as a landmark of taste and style."

The opening ceremonies began in lavish style with an invite-only event co-hosted by photographer and environmentalist Sebastian Copeland in partnership with *Vanity Fair* magazine, and attended by actors Orlando Bloom and Rosario Dawson. That evening, Vdara's employees became the first to walk through the hotel's doors. "Vdara's management have completed all of the pre-opening activities and have readied the hotel to open," said Bobby Baldwin,

ARIA's VIP opening gala included a fireworks display that illuminated its glass curtain wall with brilliant color.

Veer Towers' yellow glass façades shimmer as
the sun sets on CityCenter Drive.

president and CEO of CityCenter. "Their excitement and enthusiasm defy description as they await the opportunity to welcome the first hotel guests and residents."

More than five hundred guests attended the ribbon-cutting show for Mandarin Oriental two days later, with a program that included Taiko drummers, dancers, and a ceremony by feng shui master David Cho to promote good luck, balance, and harmony. General Manager Rajesh Jhingon came to the United States after four-and-a-half years in charge at Mandarin Oriental, Singapore, and brought to Las Vegas a thorough knowledge of the hotel's brand and standards. "What I have sought after my entire career is to work with the best brands, which deliver incredible service and a promise—and live up to that," he says. "To do something in a world-class city, with some of the finest offerings, be they food and beverage, gaming, or retail; to be part of that is great. Topping it is CityCenter, which I think will redefine Las Vegas in many, many ways. For me to represent the Mandarin, and lead the team here, is not only an honor, but also a great opportunity. There is so much happening—I wouldn't miss it for the world."

Personalized service is a hallmark of Mandarin Oriental, where the valet-only arrival experience sets the tone with no wait, and an escort up to the twenty-third-floor main lobby. When guests reach the desk, they are greeted by name, and the receptionist has in hand their preferences and requests from previous visits, which are then distributed among staff members. As directed by the Mandarin Oriental's customer-service guide, "Legendary Quality Experiences," employees do not point; instead, they escort guests to their destination.

Left to right: Angela Lester, general manager at Vdara; Bobby Baldwin, president and CEO of CityCenter; Jim Murren, CEO of MGM MIRAGE; William Grounds, president and COO of Infinity World Development; and William McBeath, president of ARIA, cut the ribbon at Vdara on December 1, 2009.

Jim Murren, CEO of MGM MIRAGE, addresses the press at the opening ceremony for ARIA, December 16, 2009: "ARIA and CityCenter reflect a combination of innovation, energy, and visionary design that we believe will reshape how the world views the destination resort experience and attract visitors from around the globe as a landmark of taste and style."

CityCenter architects meet the press on ARIA's opening day. Left to right: J. F. Finn, principal and managing director at Gensler; Paul Katz, managing principal at Kohn Pedersen Fox; Rafael Viñoly, founding principal of Rafael Viñoly Architects; Andrew Cohen, managing principal at Gensler; Art Gensler, founder and chairman of Gensler; Francisco Gonzalez-Pulido, partner at Murphy/Jahn Architects; Ko Makabe, senior designer at Kohn Pedersen Fox; Eugene Kohn, founding principal of Kohn Pedersen Fox; Dave Mexico, principal of Rockwell Group; David Rockwell, founding principal of Rockwell Group; Carla Swickerath, CEO and principal of Studio Daniel Libeskind; Daniel Libeskind, founding principal of Studio Daniel Libeskind; Gregg Jones, principal at Pelli Clarke Pelli Architects; Cesar Pelli, founding partner of Pelli Clarke Pelli Architects; and Fred Clarke, senior principal at Pelli Clarke Pelli Architects.

Award-winning chefs are introduced at CityCenter on opening day. Left to right: Jean-Philippe Maury, executive pastry chef at ARIA; Todd English of Todd English P.U.B.; Shawn McClain of Sage; Masayoshi Takayama of Shaboo/Bar Masa: Sirio Maccioni of Sirio Ristorante; Jean-Georges Vongerichten of Jean Georges Steakhouse; Julian Serrano of Julian Serrano; and Michael Mina of American Fish.

Guests enjoy afternoon tea and skyline views at Mandarin Oriental's Zen-inspired Tea Lounge.

Upon arrival at their rooms, guests enter via keyless locks, and control lights, temperature, and entertainment systems from automated control panels. Staff telephones are answered no later than the third ring, and baggage must be delivered—and guest complaints dealt with—within ten minutes. Every room service order, from a cup of coffee to a three-course meal, arrives with a surprise perk such as a cookie. "For us, luxury is about acknowledging the individual, irrespective of purchasing power at the casino," says Jhingon. "There is no cut-and-dried formula; these are small things, and easy for our colleagues to do."

The Mandarin Oriental's dining and beverage options include three-star Michelin chef Pierre Gagnaire's first restaurant in the United States, Twist; all-day service at Asian-inspired MOzen Bistro; the intimate Tea Lounge; and the twenty-third-floor Mandarin Bar, noted for its stunning views. For formal gatherings, the third floor's Oriental Ballroom, Lotus and Jade rooms, 3,000-sq.-ft. pre-function area, private meeting rooms, and custom-designed boardroom comprise more than 12,000 sq. ft. and come equipped with the latest technology systems. Whether for twenty people or four hundred, the hotel's dedicated event-planning team insures that each business or social event displays Mandarin Oriental's signature attention to detail.

For those who wish to experience the hotel's restaurants, spa, fitness center, and service on a more permanent basis, Mandarin Oriental's 225 luxury residences are among the most exclusive addresses on the Strip. Residents enjoy a dedicated concierge and staff, plus a private entrance, lobby area, elevator, and parking garage. Most of all, they receive a level of service that can only be attained through mutual familiarity. "Part of the Mandarin's promise is to deliver a fantastic lifestyle, a personalized service, and dedicated facilities for the residences," says Jhingon. "Having the residents be able to access the hotel's services at their own pace, for us to get to know them better, for us to get to know our residents, their likes and dislikes, and be able to translate that into the actual delivery of service, with the perfect recognition, that is part of the Mandarin experience, That is something we have done very well in Mandarins worldwide."

In late 2005 MGM MIRAGE recruited Tony Dennis, formerly of the Four Seasons Resorts and Hotel group, as executive vice president of CityCenter's Residential Division. Dennis's mission was to develop, market, and operate the 2,400 condo-hotel and condo units at Mandarin Oriental, Vdara, and Veer Tow-

1 The residential sales office conducts private viewings of the residences, supplemented by scaled models, floor plans, and "Living in the Details" community guides, which help to build an accurate picture of life at CityCenter and in Las Vegas at large.

2 CityCenter's residential sales office on Las Vegas Boulevard is the first stop for prospective buyers at the Residences at Mandarin Oriental, Vdara, and Veer Towers.

1. Concierge staff members are stationed on the first floor of Crystals' three-story treehouse structure to organize personal shopping appointments and consultations.

2. The Porsche Design Group's Crystals store—its fifth in the U.S.—carries the exclusive Austrian brand's full line of technically inspired men's accessories, watches, fragrances, and sport and fashion collections.

3. Luxury brand Bulgari brings its signature Italian style to Crystals with a "twin" concept store that divides jewelry and watches from accessories and fine leather goods. A connecting corridor resembles a traditional "Campidoglio" (Roman square), complete with floor-to-ceiling fountain.

4. Tiffany & Co.'s elegant Crystals store faces the Strip with an 85-ft.-high diamond-shaped façade, befitting the iconic jeweler. Through its Art Deco–inspired doors, the 10,000-sq.-ft., 2-story space features a crystalline stone and glass spiral staircase, lit from beneath, a curved, multilayered ceiling, crystal-covered walls, and private sales salons.

ers, whose revenues were vital to offset CityCenter's initial costs. Based on the scale of the development and residential market trends, Dennis predicted a 66 percent regional, 20 percent local, and 14 percent international sales breakdown. MGM MIRAGE utilized its pre-existing database of business relationships for the marketing campaign, which exceeded expectations by delivering 30 percent local original purchasers. "There are three reasons why people from these locales might buy: for their personal use, as an investment vehicle, or as a part-time home. So it was those three buckets from which we expected to draw demand to fill the residences," he says.

Benchmarking studies of residential projects from Miami to San Diego informed the number of units per building, interior design, layout, amenities, and finishes. Market absorption rates and sell-out times were key considerations, as CityCenter's atmosphere and long-term growth depended on population. The condo-hotel was new to the market, so MGM MIRAGE looked to the suc-cesses of others, and to its own Signature property, to develop the optimum mix of studios, penthouses, and one-, two-, and three-bedrooms. "So that was instrumental in the developmental stages in helping us plan the product and helping us to estab-lish our financial expectations as well as price positioning, and who the customers would likely be so we could match all that up to our own expectations and projections and relationships," says Dennis.

At 18 million sq. ft., CityCenter is the larg-est urban district to be built in its entirety, ahead of the Olympic Village in China. "If you think CityCenter was built for 2011, you are mistaken—it was built for 2020 or 2030," says Dennis. "CityCenter is going to be the center of the city within the city, but it may take the city time to grow into that frame-work; that is how I see it. It is unrealistic

One of Crystals' first prospective tenants, fine jeweler and watchmaker Harry Winston set a new benchmark for the brand with a 1,800-sq.-ft concept store by New York architect William Sofield.

to think that you could mix everything and just plug in and play. The reality of development on this scale is that it takes time to bring it to its fullest potential."

On December 3, 2009, select shoppers previewed thirty-six of Crystals' shops and restaurants at a noon charity shopping event before the retail center officially opened to the public at 5 p.m. CityCenter's retail line-up set the tone for the development, with the world's most recognizable upscale brands located side by side in a setting that surpassed all shopping-center precedents in scale, design, circulation, and ambition. Names such as Louis Vuitton and Tiffany were well established in Las Vegas, but Crystals added more to their repertoires than just beautiful stores. "They had never operated or designed something within this kind of architectural environment," says Frank Visconti, president of MGM MIRAGE Retail Operations. "And they stepped up and created something unique and very different."

At three stories high, the Louis Vuitton Crystals flagship is its largest in North America and a formidable embossed-stainless-steel presence on the Strip. The French design house is one of the most visible brands in the world, selling luxury clothing, luggage, jewelry, and accessories at 461 dedicated stores in 50 countries. A Las Vegas staple since 1988, it opened first at Fashion Mall before expanding to casino locations Caesars Palace, the Wynn, and Bellagio.

Crystals has proved a commercial as well as an architectural success, with a steady rise in retail revenues. However, it was not fully occupied on opening day, when consumer confidence was at its lowest in decades. Among the retailers who bet big—and early—on Crystals was fine jeweler and watchmaker Harry Winston, a company born against enormous odds. Founded in New York in 1932, at the height of the Great Depression, the brand currently has twenty-two prestigious locations around the globe. At Crystals, Harry Winston set a new benchmark for the brand with a 1,800-sq.-ft concept store by New York architect William Sofield. Its transparent, diamond-like façade, salon environment, and grand black and white marble entrance will be the blueprint for future outlets worldwide, starting with Shanghai, China.

According to Frédéric de Narp, president and CEO at Harry Winston, Crystals was the right place, and the timing was entirely in keeping with the brand. "Harry Winston was a fearless visionary, genius, who created Harry Winston the brand in the worst depression in U.S. history," he says. "When we considered opening our salon at the exceptional CityCenter Crystals retail center during the recession, we did not fear the short-term crisis, but found the long-term prospects quite appealing. Like Crystals, we make no compromise on quality or on the company we keep."

ARIA Resort & Casino welcomed its first guests on the evening of December 16 with a VIP invite-only opening gala and a fireworks display that illuminated its glass curtain wall with brilliant color. Locals gathered outside, and entered the resort shortly before midnight for their first glimpse of CityCenter's centerpiece. "If you look at any mixed-use development, there is usually an anchor tenant," says William McBeath, president of ARIA, "and ARIA is the anchor tenant, the backdrop that gives credibility to everything else and promotes exploration and discovery, and draws people in with its scale, its movement, its architectural lines and the shiny glass. It beckons people to come see what is inside, and the fact that it promotes discovery and exploration and creates circulation for the benefit of the rest of the business was clearly contemplated and a core part of the program."

McBeath came to ARIA with a long Las Vegas career, beginning within Steve Wynn's Mirage group in 1986. At the time of the MGM MIRAGE merger, McBeath was president and CEO of Treasure Island, and in 2005, he became both president of Bellagio and an integral part of the CityCenter team. McBeath cites legendary stickler Walt Disney, who once banned chewing gum from his parks because of the mess it creates, as a strong influence on his management style. "When Walt Disney was a little kid, he saw this beautiful merry-go-round and his father finally took him to it," McBeath says. "He was just so enamored with the movement, the articulation of the moving horses, and all the different color palettes that he paid his fare and got on. When it was moving from far away it looked fine, but up close it was dilapidated, with chipped paint, and half the horses did not go up and down. Walt had a very simple motto: 'No chipped paint, and all the horses move.'"

ARIA passes the closest of scrutiny with a unique back-of-house design that conceals all trash removal, deliveries, linen and laundry services, and a 100,000 sq. ft. warehouse that supports 20,000 meals per day. Staff services the hotel with minimal disruption to guests via a complex series of subterranean tunnels, including a 750-ft. passageway to transport linens to and from the pool

New York–based hospitality designer Therese Virserius Design envisioned Bar Vdara as the jewel of the hotel, reflected in its palette of fuchsia, gold, purple, green, orange, and magenta, luxurious upholstery, and striped-marble bar top. Located on the lobby floor, its four distinct areas form one continuous space: the interior bar and lounge are divided from the upper and lower outdoor seating areas by sheer panels during the day, while darker separations create a greater sense of intimacy in the evening.

Among the attractions at Bar Vdara's lower outdoor lounge are deep-seated couches, an under-lit infinity pool, garden swings that seat up to six people, and views of Nancy Rubins' 57-ft.-tall steel-and-aluminum sculpture *Big Edge* (right). The more intimate outdoor seating area is enclosed by custom-made planters.

1   With easy access to the casino floor, ARIA's full-service City Bar offers a relaxed retreat from gaming twenty-four hours a day amid crackled greenish blue glass and dark wood.

2   Located on ARIA's Promenade level, Jean Georges Steakhouse is a contemporary take on the traditional steakhouse by Michelin three-star, James Beard Award–winning chef Jean-Georges Vongerichten. New York–based firm Dupoux Design divided the amphitheater-inspired restaurant into a sophisticated lounge, elevated dining areas, and a private chef's–table room.

3   ARIA's Lemongrass is the first Thai restaurant to be housed in a major resort on the Strip. Designed by New York- and Bangkok-based firm AvroKO, it comprises a 100-seat dining room and a 51-seat lounge, where guests can enjoy cocktails and teas or a full meal. Inspired by a traditional Thai silk factory, the restaurant's elegant yet unpretentious interiors combine lush fabrics, bold colors, textures, and industrial materials. Chef Krairavee, formerly of Le Fenix Hotel in Bangkok, presents that city's contemporary flavors alongside renditions of classic dishes. The dining room features an interactive satay bar, where poultry, pork, and seafood are char-grilled over an open fire.

café VETTRO

4
+
5 Designed by Bentel & Bentel, Café Vettro spans ARIA's north face, behind a 40-ft.-high silk-embedded glass curtain wall. With 600 seats, it is the largest 24-hour café and restaurant in Las Vegas and incorporates reclaimed stone from the iconic Boardwalk Hotel, which stood where CityCenter is now.

6 Designed by Jean-Philippe Maury and New York City firm Norwood Oliver Design Associates, ARIA's Jean Philippe Patisserie's 85-seat café offers a 45-flavor line of house-made gelato, crêpes, sandwiches, and salads, as well as gourmet bonbons and chocolate truffles.

Located on ARIA's Casino level, Jean Philippe Patisserie is the sequel to chef Jean-Philippe Maury's first Parisian-style pastry shop at the Bellagio, which opened in 2005 and boasts the world's largest chocolate fountain.

ARIA's VIP opening gala included a fireworks display that illuminated its glass curtain wall with brilliant color.

deck. No service vehicles are allowed on grade at CityCenter, and all taxis and limousines queue from underground and immediately re-enter an underground tunnel. To limit exhaust fumes and congestion, all passenger vehicles are strictly drop-off only in arrival areas.

As the largest resort at CityCenter, ARIA flies the flag for the development's environmentally conscious approach to design and operations. The resort commissioned a fleet of twenty-nine compressed natural gas (CNG) stretch limousines, used primarily for roundtrip airport transportation for patrons of its Sky Suites hotel-within-a-hotel and neighboring Vdara Hotel & Spa. Without forfeiting luxury, the 24-ft.-long Lincoln Town Cars release 90–97 percent fewer

ARIA's Sage restaurant awaits its first diners on opening day. Designed by French architect Jacques Garcia, it is the first restaurant outside the Midwest for Chef Shawn McClain, owner of Chicago eateries Spring, Green Zebra, and Custom House. McClain's globally influenced American menu is served amid Garcia's opulent muted-gold pillars, tiled walls, plum-colored drapery and furniture, and deep-stained wood flooring.

CityCenter Drive bustles with activity after opening day.

toxic emissions than conventional gasoline- and diesel- powered cars. Inside the hotel, "smart sensor" technology detects when rooms are vacant and automatically turns off lights and electronics, while the spa—like all at CityCenter—uses only natural and organic oils. ARIA's casino features 1,940 slot machines, all of which contain energy-efficient LED bulbs and bases that act as displacement ventilation units.

Environmental sustainability at ARIA sets a model not only for CityCenter but also for MGM MIRAGE at large. "It all happened at the same time—my job was parallel," says Cindy Ortega, the firm's senior vice president of Energy and Environmental Services. "As best practices in CityCenter were articulated by the architects and engineers, we integrated these practices into all of our operations. As we planned environmentally sustainable operations for ARIA, we inte-

grated those practices into our other resorts. So we were greening the entire company at the same we were completing ARIA."

In keeping with the "green" theme, ARIA's guest rooms, Sky Suites, and public spaces are home to approximately 300 seasonal trees, which spend three months at a time in the resort. While many Las Vegas hotels use Kentia or Rhapis palms, which require little sunlight, Richard Honzo, director of horticulture at ARIA, specified a variety of Yuccas, Aralias and Dracenas—rare sights indoors. Every three months, before they begin to decline, the trees are rotated to CityCenter's nearby greenhouse to recover and are replaced with a waiting set. "A lot of the higher-end Las Vegas hotels have trees throughout to give a beautiful atmosphere," says Honzo, director of horticulture at ARIA. "It is not a very good practice, because you take a tree

CityCenter retained eight separate consultants to create building and directional signage for pedestrians and vehicles.

ARIA's 80,000-sq.-ft., two-level spa complex creates a calm and tranquil atmosphere through the use of salt, stone, earth, and fire. Guests first experience the stone and water garden, adorned with sacred Japanese Aji stones, before transitioning to sixty-two individual treatment rooms or three spa suites, which can accommodate couples or small groups.

that requires natural light conditions and you place it in a casino, where it eventually dies, and then you throw it out and replace it with a new tree. It is a vicious cycle, and not a practice we wanted to start at our hotel."

William McBeath, ARIA President, resided at ARIA for the first sixty days of operations, during which he immersed himself in every aspect of the resort, from its restaurants and stores to the gaming areas and convention center. But most importantly, McBeath put a face on ARIA's leadership, holding pep rallies with Jim Murren and Bobby Baldwin for the hotel's 3,000+ employees. "I believe that my single greatest role is to create an environment where people feel valued and secure," says McBeath. "When people feel valued, their productivity is that much higher, and they can focus on what they are supposed to do—service the guest—without worrying about the boss."

The morning of December 16 began with an 11 a.m. press conference, held by MGM MIRAGE and Infinity Development Corp. executives, CityCenter's architects, designers, and creative partners, and U.S. Green Building Council president, CEO, and founding chair, Rick Fedrizzi. Speakers included Jim Murren; Bobby Baldwin; William Grounds, president of Infinity World Development; Cesar Pelli, architect at ARIA; and Rick Fedrizzi. To mark CityCenter's creation of 12,000 permanent jobs—the single largest hiring effort in the country—senior executives from both MGM MIRAGE and Infinity World had the honor of remotely ringing the closing bell of the New York Stock Exchange from the Mandarin Terrace.

For Jim Murren, what began as a collection of diagrams and sketches was now a reality. And like all great achievements, it had often seemed impossible. "CityCenter symbolizes the tremendous quality of humans: resolve, bravery, courage, and determination, and staring down adversity," he says. "I doubt the many millions who wander through Central Park know how ridiculed and how controversial a project such as that was in its time. It is hard to capture the energy that went into building something like CityCenter; it is a story that most people won't know, and that is fine. I just hope that when they see what has been created here, they enjoy it."

Interior of Crystals with its segmented ceiling lines and angular skylights. The David Rockwell-designed *Treehouse* is the background.

Acknowledgments

This book project began with a fortuitous introduction by KPF Chairman and architect A. Eugene Kohn. On March 4, 2010, Gene taught a class at Harvard Business School that featured case studies of CityCenter and guest speaker Bill Smith, President of MGM MIRAGE Design Group. After class, Gene introduced Bill to author and book producer Scott Tilden and suggested they collaborate on a CityCenter book.

After choosing to collaborate, we secured approval from MGM Resorts International and signed an agreement with W. W. Norton & Company to publish *Creating CityCenter*. We want to pay tribute to all the people who helped develop CityCenter and made this book possible.

First and foremost, we would like to thank Jim Murren, Chairman and CEO of MGM Resorts International, for conceiving the CityCenter development and championing this book. Bobby Baldwin, President and CEO of CityCenter Holdings, LLC, and Director of MGM Resorts International, headed development of CityCenter, granted an interview for the book, underwrote its writing and approved its photography. Frank Visconti, President of MGM Resorts International Retail and Crystals shopping facility at CityCenter, granted an interview and handled contract compliance and payments for the book project. His accounting director, Doreen Kaz, was also most helpful.

Tom Reich, Bruce Aguilera, and April Chaparian of MGM Resorts International steered the book project through the transcript approval process. Jenn Michaels, Vice President of Public Relations for MGM Resorts International, provided additional support in reviewing transcripts and texts for the book. Jon Schmidt provided many of the highly detailed photographs and coordinated the selection of images and their transfer to the publisher. Vickie McCoy handled many critical and time-consuming details in the creation of this book, including transcript and photography approvals.

We would especially like to thank Lynne Lavelle for turning a rough manuscript into a beautifully crafted text. And last but not least, we appreciate the time and dedication of Nancy Green, the acquiring editor for our book. Her belief in the book never waned. Nancy was committed to telling the CityCenter story to a broad audience.

Scott Tilden also wishes to thank the following individuals who granted him interviews and provided invaluable insights on their firms' role on the CityCenter project.

Robert F. Baker	President of Baker Metal Products, 11/18/2011
Robert Baldwin	President and CEO of CityCenter Holdings, LLC, and Chief Design and Construction Officer and Director of MGM Resorts International, 5/17/2011
Peter A. Bentel	Partner of Bentel and Bentel, 10/18/2011
Jereck Boss	Principal of Office of James Burnett, 11/16/2011
Michael Burke	CEO of Bulgari, 3/9/12
Yves Carcelle	former CEO of Louis Vuitton, 1/20/12
Peter Cavaluzzi	Principal of Ehrenkrantz Eckstut and Kuhn, 6/17/2011
Andy Cohen	Executive Director of Gensler, 7/29/2011
David Cooper	President of WSP Flack and Kurtz, 11/18/2011
James Corner	Principal, and Elizabeth Fain LaBombard, Associate of James Corner Field Operations, 7/29/2011
Daniel J. D'Arrigo	Executive Vice President, CFO, and Treasurer of MGM Resorts International, 11/18/2011
Tony Dennis	Executive Vice President of CityCenter, 5/27/2011
Chris Fannin	formerly Managing Partner at D.I.R.T. Studio and now Director of Planning for Asia Pacific of HOK, 11/18/2011
William Grounds	President of Infinity World Development, 10/27/2011
George Hargreaves	Senior Principal, and Brian Jencek, Principal of Hargreaves Associates, 10/19/2011
Richard Honzo	Director of Horticulture of Aria Resort & Casino, 12/02/2011
Helmut Jahn	CEO, and Francisco Gonzalez-Pulido, President of JAHN, 6/8/2011
David Jansen	Principal of Adamson Associates, 11/01/2011
Eugene Kohn	Chairman of Kohn Pedersen Fox, 6/23/2011
Guy Laliberté	CEO of Cirque du Soleil, 5/17/2011
Kay Lang	President and CEO of Kay Lang + Associates, 6/30/2011
William McBeath	President and COO of Aria Resort & Casino, 10/27/2011
Shawn McCLain	Executive Chef of Sage at Aria Resort & Casino, 1/18/2012
Daniel P. McQuade	CEO of Tishman Construction Corporation, 10/17/2011
James Murren	Chairman and CEO of MGM Resorts International, 5/31/2011
Frédéric de Narp	CEO and President of Harry Winston, Inc., 1/30/12
Cindy Ortega	Senior Vice President Energy and Environmental Services of MGM Resorts International, 6/28/2011
Cesar Pelli	Senior Principal, Fred W. Clarke, Senior Principal, and Gregg E. Jones, Principal of Pelli Clarke Pelli, 6/14/2011
Peter Remedios	President and Managing Principal of Remedios Studio, Inc., 10/24/2011
Julian Serrano	Executive Chef of Julian Serrano at Aria Resort & Casino, 1/12/12
Adam D. Tihany	President of Tihany Design, 6/15/11
Sven Van Assche	Senior Vice President Design of MGM Resorts International, 6/15/2011
Frank Visconti	President of MGM Resorts International Retail & Crystals at CityCenter, 6/30/2011

Photography Credits

D.I.R.T. Studio: 173

Ehrenkrantz, Eckstut + Kuhn: 46, 49 (upper right)

Gensler: 136, 137 (bottom left)

Jahn: 141, 143, 144

James Corner Field Operations: 177

KPF: 90, 91

Las Vegas Convention and Visitors Authority: 10, 12, 15,16, 18, 19, 20, 21, 22

Mandarin Oriental: 87, 89, 92, 94, 95, 98 100, 101, 192

MGM Resorts International: 17, 23, 24, 27, 32, 33

Pelli Clarke Pelli: 106, 107, 108, 109

Perini: 128 (bottom)

Rafael Vinoly Architects: 4, 5, 152 (bottom middle), 153 (left), 154, 155

Robert A. M. Stern Architects: 44 (top), 45 (top left)

Rockwell Group: 134

SK+G Advertising/Scott Frances: 2, 3, 6, 9, 28 34, 35, 38, 50, 52, 53, 97, 104, 105, 113, 116, 118, 119, 120, 121, 122, 123 (bottom right), 124, 127, 137 (bottom right), 139, 142, 146 (bottom right), 150, 156, 157, 161, 162 (right), 163, 164, 165, 174, 175, 184, 185, 188, 189, 198, 199, 200, 201, 202, 203 (top left, top middle, bottom left), 207, 210, 211, 213, 214, 215, 217

Studio Daniel Libeskind: 129 (bottom left, bottom right), 131 (right), 132, 133

Tishman Construction Corp: 63 (bottom left)

Visions in Photography: 58, 59, 64 (top left, top right), 68, 69

Harry Winston: 195

INDEX